First World War
and Army of Occupation
War Diary
France, Belgium and Germany

16 DIVISION
47 Infantry Brigade
Prince of Wales's Leinster Regiment (Royal Canadians)
7th Battalion
16 December 1915 - 23 January 1918

WO95/1970/4

The Naval & Military Press Ltd
www.nmarchive.com
Published in association with The National Archives

Published by

The Naval & Military Press Ltd

Unit 10 Ridgewood Industrial Park,

Uckfield, East Sussex,

TN22 5QE England

Tel: +44 (0) 1825 749494

www.naval-military-press.com

www.nmarchive.com

This diary has been reprinted in facsimile from the original. Any imperfections are inevitably reproduced and the quality may fall short of modern type and cartographic standards.

© **Crown Copyright**
Images reproduced by permission of The National Archives, London, England, 2015.

Contents

Document type	Place/Title	Date From	Date To
Heading	WO95/1790, 16 Div-47 Inf Bde 7 Leinster Regt Dec 1915-Feb1918		
Heading	7th Br Leinster Regiment		
Heading	15th Division 47th Infy Bde 7th Bn Leinster Regt Dec 1915-Feb 1918		
Heading	16th Division 7th Leicester Rgt. Vol I		
War Diary	Farn Borough	16/12/1915	16/12/1915
War Diary	Southampton	17/12/1915	17/12/1915
War Diary	Haure	18/12/1915	25/12/1915
War Diary	Billets	25/12/1915	25/12/1915
War Diary	Philosophe	26/12/1915	26/12/1915
War Diary	Gosnay	26/12/1915	27/12/1915
War Diary	Verquin	27/12/1915	27/12/1915
War Diary	Gosnay	27/12/1915	27/12/1915
War Diary	Minx	27/12/1915	27/12/1915
War Diary	Gosnay	28/12/1915	30/12/1915
War Diary	Laires	30/12/1915	31/12/1915
Heading	7th Leinsters Vol. 2		
War Diary	Laires	01/01/1916	03/01/1916
War Diary	Lisbourg	04/01/1916	04/01/1916
War Diary	Coupelle-Neuve	05/01/1916	06/01/1916
War Diary	Coupelle Neuve	07/01/1916	07/01/1916
War Diary	Laires	08/01/1916	14/01/1916
War Diary	Lapugnoy	14/01/1916	15/01/1916
War Diary	Houchin	15/01/1916	16/01/1916
War Diary	S.Maroc	17/01/1916	17/01/1916
War Diary	Loos Sector	17/01/1916	17/01/1916
War Diary	Maroc Sector	17/01/1916	17/01/1916
War Diary	S.Maroc	18/01/1916	18/01/1916
War Diary	Loos	18/01/1916	18/01/1916
War Diary	S.Maroc. Loos	19/01/1916	24/01/1916
War Diary	Lesbrebis	25/01/1916	27/01/1916
War Diary	Noeux-Les-Mines	27/01/1916	27/01/1916
War Diary	Marles-Les-Mines	27/01/1916	28/01/1916
War Diary	Livossart & Palfart	29/01/1916	31/01/1916
Miscellaneous	Copy of Letter From G.O.C. 141st Inf Bde to Major General Commanding 47th Division	17/01/1916	17/01/1916
Heading	16 Div 47 Bde 7th Leinster Regt 1917 Nov-Dec		
Heading	Battle Dress Question Naire		
Heading	War Diary of 7th (S) Bn The Leinster 4th From 4th February To 29th February 1916 Volume II		
War Diary	Palfart Livossart A.13.b.36B	04/02/1916	06/02/1916
War Diary	Nedon Nedon Nedonchelle	06/02/1916	08/02/1916
War Diary	Marles-Les-Mines	08/02/1916	09/02/1916
War Diary	Bethune	09/02/1916	10/02/1916
War Diary	Annequin La Bassee	11/02/1916	12/02/1916
War Diary	Bethune	13/02/1916	13/02/1916
War Diary	Cambrin	14/02/1916	17/02/1916
War Diary	Nedon Nedonchelle	18/02/1916	18/02/1916
War Diary	Livossart Palfart Mont Cornet	19/02/1916	29/02/1916

War Diary	Norrente-Fontes (N.35.b.Sheet 36)	29/02/1916	08/03/1916
War Diary	Allouagne (C.7.a Sheet 36 B)	09/03/1916	18/03/1916
War Diary	Allouagne	19/03/1916	25/03/1916
War Diary	Noeux-Les-Mines	25/03/1916	25/03/1916
War Diary	Puits 14 BIS	26/03/1916	31/03/1916
War Diary	Noeux-Les-Mines	01/04/1916	06/04/1916
War Diary	Philosophe	07/04/1916	09/04/1916
War Diary	Tenth Avenue	09/04/1916	12/04/1916
War Diary	Left Subsection Hulluch	12/04/1916	20/04/1916
War Diary	Mazingarbe	20/04/1916	28/04/1916
War Diary	Philosophe	29/04/1916	29/04/1916
War Diary	Right Subsection Hulluch	29/04/1916	04/05/1916
War Diary	Philosophe East	04/05/1916	10/05/1916
War Diary	Left Q Puits 14 BIS	11/05/1916	11/05/1916
War Diary	Puits No B12	12/05/1916	12/05/1916
War Diary	Puits No 14 B15	15/05/1916	16/05/1916
War Diary	Left Sub Section	17/05/1916	17/05/1916
War Diary	Noeux-Les-Mines.	18/05/1916	25/05/1916
War Diary	Philosophe West	25/05/1916	29/05/1916
War Diary	Left Sub Section	29/05/1916	06/06/1916
War Diary	Duits 14 B15	07/06/1916	07/06/1916
War Diary	Bde Support	08/06/1916	11/06/1916
War Diary	Mazingarbe	11/06/1916	17/06/1916
War Diary	Bde Support	18/06/1916	21/06/1916
War Diary	Right Sub Section Loos	22/06/1916	26/06/1916
War Diary	Brigade Support	27/06/1916	30/06/1916
Heading	War Diary 7th (S) Bn The Leinster Rgt 1st. July To 31st. July 1916. Volume. 8		
War Diary	Right Subsection Loos	01/07/1916	03/07/1916
War Diary	Noeux-Les-Mines	04/07/1916	10/07/1916
War Diary	Left Sub Section Duits 14 B15	11/07/1916	15/07/1916
War Diary	Laigade Reserve Philosophe	15/07/1916	19/07/1916
War Diary	Left Subsection Puits 14 B15	20/07/1916	25/07/1916
War Diary	Brigade Reserve Philosophe	26/07/1916	30/07/1916
War Diary	Mazingarbe	31/07/1916	31/07/1916
Heading	War Diary 7th Leinster Regiment Month Of August, 1916 Volume 9		
Miscellaneous	H.9 47th Bde	13/09/1916	13/09/1916
War Diary	Left-Sub-Section Loos	10/08/1916	13/08/1916
War Diary	Brigade Support	14/08/1916	17/08/1916
War Diary	Left Sub Section Loos	18/08/1916	31/08/1916
Heading	War Diary 7th Leinster Regiment Month Of September 1916 Volume 10		
War Diary	In The Field	01/09/1916	30/09/1916
Heading	War Diary Month Of October , 1916 Volume 11 7th Leinster Regiment		
War Diary	In The Field	01/10/1916	31/10/1916
Heading	War Diary For Month Of November, 1916 Volume 12 7th Leinster Regiment		
War Diary	In The Field	01/11/1916	30/11/1916
Heading	War Diary For Month Of December, 1916. Volume 13 7th Leinster Regiment		
War Diary	In The Field	01/12/1916	31/12/1916
Heading	War Diary For Month Of January, 1917 Volume 14 7th Btn Leinster Regiment		
War Diary	Spam Broek Sector	01/01/1917	04/01/1917

War Diary	Derry Huts	05/01/1917	13/01/1917
War Diary	Spam Broer Sector	14/01/1917	31/01/1917
Heading	War Diary For Month Of February, 1917 Volume15 7th Leinster Regiment		
War Diary	In The Field	01/02/1917	28/02/1917
Heading	War Diary For Month Of March, 1917 Volume 16 Unit-7th Btn Leinster Regiment		
War Diary	Kemmel Shelters	01/03/1917	01/03/1917
War Diary	Doctors House Kemmel	02/03/1917	02/03/1917
War Diary	Bde Support	03/03/1917	05/03/1917
War Diary	Right Sub Section	06/03/1917	31/03/1917
Heading	War Diary For Month Of April, 1917. Volume 17 Unit:- 7th Leinster Regiment		
War Diary		01/04/1917	30/04/1917
Heading	War Diary Volume:- 18 For Month Of May, 1917 Unit:- 7th Leinster Regiment		
War Diary		01/05/1917	31/05/1917
Heading	War Diary For Month Of June, 1917.Volume:- 19 Unit:- 7th Btn Leinster Regiment		
War Diary	In The Field	01/06/1917	30/06/1917
Miscellaneous	Headquarters 16th (Irish) Division. G.O.C., 47th Infantry Brigade	25/06/1917	25/06/1917
Miscellaneous Map	7th. Battn. Leinster Regiment.	04/06/1917	04/06/1917
Heading	War Diary For Month Of July, 1917 Volume:- 20 Unit:- 7th Leinster Regiment		
War Diary	Eringhem	01/07/1917	14/07/1917
War Diary	Eringhem Tatinghem	15/07/1917	18/07/1917
War Diary	Tatinghem	19/07/1917	22/07/1917
War Diary	Winnezeele	21/07/1917	24/07/1917
War Diary	Watou	25/07/1917	29/07/1917
War Diary	In The Field	30/07/1917	31/07/1917
Heading	War Diary For Month Of August, 1917 Volume 21 Unit 7th Leinster Regiment		
War Diary	In The Field	01/08/1917	26/08/1917
Map	R.E. Work. Hd. Qrs. & Forward Routes		
War Diary	In The Field	27/08/1917	31/08/1917
Heading	War Diary For Month Of August, 1917, Volume 22 Unit 7th Leinster Regiment		
War Diary	In The Field	01/09/1917	11/09/1917
War Diary	Railway Reserve	12/09/1917	15/09/1917
War Diary	Patricia Camp	16/09/1917	30/09/1917
Miscellaneous	Battalion Orders No. 143. By Major A.H. Seagrim, Commanding 7th Battalion Leinster Regiment. In The Field	21/09/1917	21/09/1917
Heading	War Diary For Month Of October, 1917.Unit 7th Leinster Regiment Volume 23		
War Diary	In The Field	01/10/1917	17/10/1917
War Diary	Patricia Camp	18/10/1917	24/10/1917
War Diary	Durrow Camp	25/10/1917	31/10/1917
Miscellaneous	Major General, G.S.	25/10/1917	25/10/1917
Heading	File No.G.12 Minor Operations. Raid By 7th Leinster Regt. 16th October, 1917	16/10/1917	16/10/1917
Miscellaneous	VI Corps 16th Div. No. A.S.1239/84	19/10/1917	19/10/1917
Miscellaneous	H.Q. VI Corps.G.X. 313/97 16th. Division	26/10/1917	26/10/1917
Miscellaneous	47th Inf. Bde. No. G. 4463. 16th Division	18/10/1917	18/10/1917

Diagram etc	Hindenburg Line		
Miscellaneous	Report On Tunnel Trench-51.b.u.20.b.	16/10/1917	16/10/1917
Miscellaneous	Enterprise By 7th Battalion Leinster Regt.	16/10/1917	16/10/1917
Heading	War Diary For Month Of November, 1917. Volume:- 24 Unit:- 7th Leinster Regiment		
War Diary	Durrow Camp	01/11/1917	02/11/1917
War Diary	In The Field	03/11/1917	18/11/1917
War Diary	Dysart Camp	19/11/1917	19/11/1917
War Diary	In The Field	20/11/1917	26/11/1917
War Diary	Durrow Camp	27/11/1917	30/11/1917
Miscellaneous		17/11/1917	17/11/1917
Miscellaneous	Janet Secret Order No.4.	17/11/1917	17/11/1917
Miscellaneous	7th Leinster Regiment	28/11/1917	28/11/1917
Map	Front Line Dispositions. RT. Battn. 47th-Inf. Bde.		
Map	Front Line Dispositions Janet. 47th Inf. Bde		
Heading	War Diary For Month Of December, 1917 Volume: 25 Unit- 7th Leinster Regiment		
War Diary	Durrow Camp	01/12/1917	02/12/1917
War Diary	Gomiecourt	02/12/1917	03/12/1917
War Diary	Beaulan Court	03/12/1917	06/12/1917
War Diary	Tincourt	07/12/1917	11/12/1917
War Diary	Front Line	12/12/1917	17/12/1917
War Diary	Stemilie	17/12/1917	22/12/1917
War Diary	Tincourt	23/12/1917	28/12/1917
War Diary	In the Line	29/12/1917	29/12/1917
War Diary	Front Line	30/12/1917	31/12/1917
Miscellaneous	Operation Order by Lieut. Col. G.A.M. Buckley D.S.O. Commanding 7th Leinster Regt.		
Miscellaneous	Operation Order No 12 By Lieut. Col. G.A.M. Buckley D.S.O. Commanding Janet.		
Miscellaneous	Operation Order No. 13. By Lieut. Colonel G.A.M. Buckley D.S.O. Commanding Janet.	16/12/1917	16/12/1917
Miscellaneous	Operation Order By Lieut Colonel G.A.M. Buckley D.S.O. Commanding 7th Battalion Leinster Regiment	22/12/1917	22/12/1917
Operation(al) Order(s)	Operation Order No 15. By Lieut Colonel G.A.M. Buckley D.S.O. Commanding 7th Battalion Leinster Regiment.	28/12/1917	28/12/1917
Heading	War Diary For Month Of January, 1918. Volume:- 26 Unit:- 7th Leinster Regiment		
War Diary	Front Line	01/01/1918	04/01/1918
War Diary	Bde. Support	05/01/1918	05/01/1918
War Diary	Ridge Reserve	05/01/1918	10/01/1918
War Diary	Tincourt (Divnl Reg.)	10/01/1918	12/01/1918
War Diary	Tincourt	13/01/1918	22/01/1918
War Diary	In Line	22/01/1918	28/01/1918
War Diary	Stilemilie	29/01/1918	31/01/1918
Operation(al) Order(s)	Battalion Order No 3. By Lieut Colonel G.A.M. Buckley, D.S.O. Commanding 7th Battalion Leinster Regiment In The Field	12/01/1918	12/01/1918
Miscellaneous	7th (S) Battalion. The Leinster Regiment.	11/01/1918	11/01/1918
Operation(al) Order(s)	7th Leinster Regiment. Order. No. 18.	09/01/1918	09/01/1918
Miscellaneous	7th Leinster Regiment.	14/01/1918	14/01/1918
Operation(al) Order(s)	Operation Order by Capt. V.J. Barrell ? Commdg. 7th Battn Leinster Regiment	21/01/1918	21/01/1918
Miscellaneous	Operation Order by Capt. V.J. Barrell ? Commdg. 7th Leinster Regiment in the Field. 27 Jany, 1918	27/01/1918	27/01/1918

Operation(al) Order(s)	7th Operation Order No.17.		
Miscellaneous	Reorganisation of Infantry Brigades.	31/01/1918	31/01/1918
Heading	War Diary For Month Of February, 1918 Volume:- 27 Unit- 7th Btn Leinster Regiment		
War Diary	Stemilie	01/02/1918	01/02/1918
War Diary	Front Line	02/02/1918	02/02/1918
War Diary	Right Sub-Section	02/02/1918	05/02/1918
War Diary	Front Line	05/02/1918	08/02/1918
War Diary	Bde.Res	09/01/1918	09/01/1918
War Diary	St. Emilie	10/01/1918	17/01/1918
War Diary	O.8.D.6.4	17/01/1918	23/01/1918
Operation(al) Order(s)	Operation Order No 22 By Lt. Col J.D. Mather Commdg 7th Leinster Regt	02/02/1918	02/02/1918
Operation(al) Order(s)	Operation Order, No.23 By Lt. Col. J.D. Mather. Commdg. 7th Leinster Regt.,	07/02/1918	07/02/1918
Miscellaneous	Officers and mebn of The Leinster Regiment		

WO95/1970

16 Div - 47 Inf Bde

7 Leinster Regt

Dec 1915 - Feb 1918

7th Bn
Leinster
Regiment

16TH DIVISION
47TH INFY BDE

7TH BN LEINSTER REGT
DEC 1915 – FEB 1918

7th Leinster Regt.
Vol I

16th Div.

Army Form C. 2118.

Dec '15
Feb '18

7th Toronto Bg.

16th Bg

WAR DIARY
or
INTELLIGENCE SUMMARY.
(Erase heading not required.)

Instructions regarding War Diaries and Intelligence
Summaries are contained in F. S. Regs., Part II.
and the Staff Manual respectively. Title pages
will be prepared in manuscript.

Place	Date	Hour	Summary of Events and Information	Remarks and references to Appendices
Farnborough	15.12.15	11:30am	1st Train. Left Farnborough carrying half Bn and half Regt. Transport. Train No X 758. Journey & entertainment good. Men well behaved. Arrived S'hampton 1:10 pm.	
-	-	12:55pm	2nd Train No X 757 left Farnborough carrying remainder Bn. Same remarks apply as above. Bgn. board last pointed to show names Capt Tillys. Found very useful. Congratulated by Lieutch. in management.	
Southampton	-	2:45pm	2nd Train Arrived Southampton.	
"	15.12.15	5pm (Approx)	Re Bn Tn sailed for HAVRE arranged as follows:— Horse-Trucks Wagons Bicycles. Transport BELLEROPHON. Carrying 7 transport Bn 72. 9. Officers 4. O.R. 254. " LA MARGUERITE " Adjutants " 11. O.R. 400. " EMPRESS QUEEN " " " 12. O.R. 296. A Journey was fine & destroyers accompanied on the trip. Arrangement for feeding the Bn by 3 separate boats was confusing though I imagine unavoidable. Re following depots for notice N.O.'s were not distributed to each ship.	
HAVRE.	16. 12.15	7. am.	Dis embarked. — An cold a but Luckily fine. Conveyances to take some our Bn. Company officers to camp. Tin came in stations. N'vals bottle should have been refilled but which we wid do in all cases. Despite cold night have been given by clean Transportation officer no men left in Hospital with Pneumonia.	
"	"	11 am.	3 Companies went to Rest Camp and one Company to Point VI at Station after no defects. Men were billeted out for the men to spend their Xmas rest - the men rest was trying as they had been armed after they had eaten dinner.	
"	"	9:30pm	Entrained in 36 Coaches - Accommodating - Men being eight left in which to sit. No baggage being left to lunch. Co. Capt. La Caude, Q.M. & Lieut A.R & Lt. Wilsche logged his Lt Foster Con aid an Canin aid Carved all money (PRS) the Captain & Co's D.D. & Co. Forms, taught No Wrom "Ch Jos" duty this Capts men - this should have been by be interest to Company officers to meet this Carefully. N.B. entrained Coo 3 Off 1725 O.R. Other Tables with Bn.	

Army Form C. 2118.

WAR DIARY
or
INTELLIGENCE SUMMARY.
(Erase heading not required.)

Instructions regarding War Diaries and Intelligence Summaries are contained in F.S. Regs., Part II. and the Staff Manual respectively. Title pages will be prepared in manuscript.

Place	Date	Hour	Summary of Events and Information	Remarks and references to Appendices
	19.12.15	—	Spent in train - Iru Elapo - passed Boulogne on to Hazebrouck + ST-OMER when we were told our destination forces fall instructions - News lectaing food.	
	"	9.40h	Detrained at CHOQUES - Detrainment good - marched off to billets - pneumonia in journey.	
	"	11.30 pm	Arrived at GOSNAY when we found in billets. No Officer met us on Emergence some difficulty was experienced Billets were allotted at Colomin. A HQ Coy village of GOSNAY. C + D Coys CHATEAU CHARTREUSE. B Coy under cover otherwise good.	
	20.12.15	5-30am	3 Off + O.R. 125 came into billets	
	"	7.am	Reveille - Nothing done all day except men defluap into billets. Received Bde orders - Telephone laid in to Companies.	
	21.12.15	—	Phone laid for Bde HQrs at VERQUIN. Men instructed in duties in billets - Reft area laid down.	
	22.12.15	6-30am	Roll Call Reveille	
		8.pm	1st Post	
		8.30pm	Roll Call	
		9.pm	Lights out.	
			Haufaine for route march.	
	23.12.15	1-pm	1st Party Consisting of Co. Adjr. 5 Officers + 18 NCO's went into Trenches via Motor bus 6 NOYELLES Ne TERMEHES. + AUKUCH for 2 days. Bombarded us morning 24th 7/52am. at 6 6th Bn LONDON Rgt.	
	25.12.15	1 pm	2nd Party Consisting 2nd in Command 5 Officers + 16 NCO's went to same trenches for 2 days. No trenches, Casualty striking cost from the Landstin - First Carr needed further supply horses.	

Army Form C. 2118.

WAR DIARY
or
INTELLIGENCE SUMMARY.
(Erase heading not required.)

Instructions regarding War Diaries and Intelligence Summaries are contained in F. S. Regs., Part II. and the Staff Manual respectively. Title pages will be prepared in manuscript.

Place	Date	Hour	Summary of Events and Information	Remarks and references to Appendices
Billets	25/12/15	8.30am	Refilling sent to Div: H.Qrs. 1 N.C.O. & 3 men for Guard. 1 N.C.O. & 25 men for fatigue - men not known packs to take shovels & picks.	
		10.15am	Christmas Day Generally Quiet - men viewed with pleasure puddings much appreciated also were very little drunkenness. Church Parade R.C. at GOSNAY. C.of.E. at H.E.S.D.I.G. NEUF.	
PHILOSOPHE	26.12.15	12 Noon	1 N.C.O. & 70 men sent to Bombing School to carr lasting 26/12/15 – 2/1/16 Major Kindly went to report to R.E. at PHILOSOPHE @ B.29.7 to arrange for the working of & fatigue party of 6 Officers & 208 O.R.	
		4 pm	8 Bomber Officers to take the party in watches. 25" 1 N.C.O. & Officer to PHILOSOPHE to look over Carried out during the night 26/27 while reserve Trenches – there was no Casualties - Care is needed to prevent men from straggling 2 new aug. left behind and from horse - three reported stragglers by day. during last their way Casual note should be made here of the importance of sending guide forward prior to Senior N.C.O. to promote the delay to any the king at Cr.Crofts joined Two stretcher were carried - this was no stretcher that were Carriers lookdown lads breeches without greatcoats	
GOSNAY		10.15am	Church as for 25th. Remainder of Bn. resting in billets. Useful time spent on Lectures in cleanliness of billets, sanitation generally.	
			Morning: Company route marching. Men retired from fatigue returned also rested during the morning.	
VERQUIN	27/12/15	3 pm	Conference at Brigade H.Qrs. VERQUIN by G.O.C. Division who following points: 1. Flags carried in Motor Cars as follows:- a. G.O.C. – Union Jack b. Army – Red & white c. Corps – Red & blue d. Division – Red	All ranks must know these intimately.

A.D.S.S./Forms/C. 2118.

Army Form C. 2118.

WAR DIARY
or
INTELLIGENCE SUMMARY.
(Erase heading not required.)

Instructions regarding War Diaries and Intelligence Summaries are contained in F. S. Regs., Part II. and the Staff Manual respectively. Title pages will be prepared in manuscript.

Place	Date	Hour	Summary of Events and Information	Remarks and references to Appendices
			2. Transport - Care of horses. Improving their standings &c	
			3. Boots - Repairs.	
			4. Salvage - Salvage to be done regimentally	
			5. Cleanliness of billets	
			6. Care of arms - Lewis Gun & Musketry	
			7. Observation - Training powers of full ranks	
			8. Map reading - Study of country & its peculiarities	
GOSNAY		2.30 pm	Owing to a slight error whereof the Signallers H.Qrs. was sent without kits in front of leading to the Comm. Officer going to H.Qrs. instead of keeping late – This spoils the record of reaching in daylight taking down messages	
		6.15 pm	O.C. C. & Adjutant attended the lecture	
MINX		a.m.	M. Horse died suddenly of heart failure	
		12 noon	1 Officer & 50 Other Ranks went to MINX to work with R.E. (S.K. St.) A Coy. & remaining & Coy.	
			do	
GOSNAY	28.12.15	9 a.m.	Weather fine – B.O.Q. found vacancy at times to fale.	
			Captains & Company Officers (routine duty) with C.O. H.Q. 12th in Command afters plate lecture. Company (routine duty), physical drill, musse – spare drill.	
			Violet Day – nothing worthy of note.	
			Weather - fine - Laundry.	
		9 pm	Checked Battn Roll with Company Officers	

Army Form C. 2118.

WAR DIARY
or
INTELLIGENCE SUMMARY.
(Erase heading not required.)

Instructions regarding War Diaries and Intelligence Summaries are contained in F.S. Regs., Part II. and the Staff Manual respectively. Title pages will be prepared in manuscript.

Place	Date	Hour	Summary of Events and Information	Remarks and references to Appendices
GOSNAY	29/10/15	7 a.m.	Fatigue party consisting of 1 Sub Lieutr, 10 N.C.O's, 500 other ranks, 6 horse grooms daily - PHILOSOPHE at G 2 b 36 b 2 proceeded to R.E. Established in blocks.	
		12 Noon	Similar party at 12 Noon. 20 off. 50 O.R. to same place.	
		9 a.m.	Mounted Paid, 1 NCO, 3 men and 3 men Rgmnt. DROSSIN and fatigue party 1 NCO + 25 men.	
		10 a.m.	Drew 165 bombs for practice purposes.	
		11.30 a.m.	Received orders that A & B & D Coys & 2 Coy HdQrts to move to another billeting area. Remainder of party spent in preparation for move cleaning billets.	
30/10/15		7 a.m.	Fatigue Party & motor lorries arrived to carry:- 1. Billeting party & advance party left behind to clean billets. 6. 20 Army new blankets & packs & canteens.	
		8.30 a.m.	Marched off to billets - new camping ground. Sheets rolled on back equipment. Marched out at following strength :- 13 Officers 956 O.R. Route via MARLES LES MINES - AUCHEL - CAUCHY A LA TOUR - FERFAY - BELLERY - AMETTES - NEDON - NEDONCHELLES - FONTAINE LES HERMANNS - FEBVIN - PALFART - LAIRES.	
			New uniform well stood the march well - may be cases of feeling out & two men were left in J Ambulance at AMETTES. FINE DAY FOR MARCH.	
LAIRES	30/10/15	5.15 p.m.	Arrived in new billets after 20 mile march - nothing worthy of note - everything ran smoothly	
LAIRES	31/10/15		Raining - men settling into billets throughout - insufficient care was taken with regard to water supply - at AMETTES - no arrangements arrangement for catching fresh water having been bought new wells have had no food until late in the day. Bac. office FEBVIN PALFART for the night only	

A.D.S.S./Forms/C. 2118.

7th Semester
vol: 2
16

WAR DIARY
or
INTELLIGENCE SUMMARY.

Army Form C. 2118.

Place	Date	Hour	Summary of Events and Information	Remarks and references to Appendices
LAIRES	1/1/16	7 a.m.	Raining - Men still fatigued - easy day in Coyagines	
		10.15 a.m.	Sent fatigue party 16 men to Bde Hdqrs to help in moving. Brigade moved to BERQUIGNY.	
MAZEROUVE	2/1/16	6.30 a.m.	Reveille	
at 1.00 am			Usual routine work continued. Very hard rain - uniform fuelled carried out Church Parade 10.15 am.	
		2.30 pm	Connected up by 'phone with Bde Hqrs AUBEROVIGNY.	
		2.40 pm	2 men sent to hospital ARMETTES - M. Gerino Case.	
		7 pm	1 Officer, 1 NCO, 10 men sent to bombing Course at LA BEUVRIERE by motor lorry.	
LAIRES	3/1/16		FINE DAY	
		5.10 pm	Received from Bde Hdqrs notice to be prepared to move to new billeting area early tomorrow. Commenced immediately to load up transport, get ready, an advance party.	
		8 pm	Received order to leave LAIRES at 11.30 a.m. "Posted" to VERCHIN.	
4/1/16		8 a.m.	Raining freely - Advance party O.in C. + O.M.S. + 4 men for Coy went n.a. billeting party. Bearing extra ammunt, Baggage + baggage guard. + 10.	
		11.30 a.m.	Marched out of LAIRES. This party also to act as Carry'g party.	
			4 NCOs & men for Coy - when we had proceeded about 2 miles in road message received that advance party that the French had got information VERCHIN and that there was no room for us	
LISBURG		12.15 pm	Halted to await further orders. Had lunch. 90th French Regr say food to Sent fatigue back to Bde Hqrs at BERQUIGNY- Magdin, Staff Captain out, Adj Major away.	
		1.50	Adjt went forward to VERCHIN. Found Magdin Staff Captain out, Adj Major away.	
		2 pm	Marched off to RUBY near diverted to march to RUBY.	
			Marched through ARDRES.	
		4.15 pm	Arrived outside RUBES. Billeted in COUPELLE-VIEILLE Rd. Adjt rode forward, found Divisional Staff Officer (DRONE) to COUPELLE-VIEILLE. No accommodation there.	

Army Form C. 2118.

WAR DIARY
or
INTELLIGENCE SUMMARY.
(Erase heading not required.)

Instructions regarding War Diaries and Intelligence Summaries are contained in F. S. Regs., Part II. and the Staff Manual respectively. Title pages will be prepared in manuscript.

Place	Date	Hour	Summary of Events and Information	Remarks and references to Appendices
COUPELLE-NEUVE	4.1.16	5.8pm	Received orders once again from St PMG to turn round and go to COUPELLE-NEUVE.	
		2.10pm	Arrived at COUPELLE-NEUVE. Found accommodation poor. Too much mire. Cannot be given to the cheeriness of our Spirits of all ranks during this trying time.	
	5.1.16		Fine day. Men resting in morning. Getting ready for inspection in afternoon by Gen. Wilson Cmdg IV Corps	
		4.15pm	Men inspected by Corps General with our Major Bentt Hickey Cmdg 16th Division. He was very pleased with the turnout. Specially congratulated Lt P. Murphy on his transport turnout. He said it was the best he had seen in the Division.	
	6.1.16		Very wet day. Nothing happened worthy of note.	
COUPELLE NEUVE	7.1.16	10.30am	Left COUPELLE NEUVE and marched via ERUBES — LUGY — BEAUMETZ LES AIRES to LAIRES where we took up an old billet. The men behaved well over the mat. Trying weather conditions. The boys were tired. Time was taken enroute and even named about	
		2pm	examine the CO and to the new Gen. HICKIES march. Gen. HICKIES met our journey to their cheery billets near much appreciated.	
LAIRES	8.1.16		Fine day. Rested all day. Generally settling up billets. Jet inspection in short Bombing School started by 16th DIVISION — Small Arms rifles in the army Training Continued in billets. Musketry on improvised range Small Arms to Bombing time at the mine FLECHINELLE. Grand fatigue for 16th DIV GRENADE SCHOOL with ammo Fine weather and heart frost. Things of the New food. Nothing worthy of note happened outside the customary routine.	
do	9.1.16 10.1.16		Received orders that the Battalion would more up to the trenches to undergo instruction attached to 47th LONDON DIVISION. Day spent in preparation for move 10.1./16 to LAVENTIE.	
	11.1.16		Motor lorries arrived & army riding pack transport necked out but LAIRES and 9 am leaving. a small transport guard behind to look after heavy baggage left behind. Clothing was not replied with the trench. Men marched light camping between one in madaction cape strapped on less of their	
do	12.1.16	10. am		

Army Form C. 211

WAR DIARY
or
INTELLIGENCE SUMMARY.
(Erase heading not required.)

Instructions regarding War Diaries and Intelligence Summaries are contained in F. S. Regs., Part II. and the Staff Manual respectively. Title pages will be prepared in manuscript.

Place	Date	Hour	Summary of Events and Information	Remarks and references to Appendices
	12.1.16 14.		Men marched well and considering the bad state of some of the boots have been very few falling out. A Battalion was accompanied by an Ambulance, who was badly needed for the 4 or 5 cases sickness on the march. Marched by FEBVIN PALFART – NEDON CHELLE – AMETTES– FERFAY– CAUCHY– A-LA-TOUR – MARLES LES MINES – LAPUGNOY. Dinners and Coffee awaited and eaten outside FERFAY.	
LAPUGNOY	13.1.16	5.10pm	Arrived at LAPUGNOY. Billets very far apart and not good, this was perhaps due in some measure to the long camping our billeting party had in locating them and their arriving rather later than they anticipated in CAUCHY.	
	15.1.16	10 a.m	After inspection of billets covering but an Service – marched from LAPUGNOY via BRUAY to HOUCHIN. Dinner cooked and eaten en route. Fine day – Cold. (KEN.M. H.2.)	
HOUCHIN	15.1.16	3.15pm	Arrived at HOUCHIN at 3.15pm. Billets good but Coy by last unit in dirty condition – billets are altogether and comfortable – Cookhouses and Canteens on Knees Rooms. Visit from D.S.O. 1. 47th DIVISION.	
	16.1.16	11 a.m	Marched out of HOUCHIN after all billets cleaned. No temps provided and men in Companies were marching under very heavy loads. Many in addition to their packs – blankets – & haversacks were to be much too heavy for men, had to fall out. Coys stopped to make a short journey to bring up stragglers. Daily learnt that great care must be taken in future. Marched via NOEUX LES MINES – MAZINGARBE & LES BREBIS – HeTeott halted in a field outside LES BREBIS at 3.30 pm and moved up by Companies in half Company starting at 3.45. The was a damp, chilly and harassed who remarkably killed by Mr Bunny. "B" Company without the first 2 Officers, who had to obtain details of the attachments. "B" Company arrived at Headquarters A. & D Coys 17th W. INF. BDE. "B" Company attached to 6 & 7 2nd LONDONS at 1/40 INF BDE. 8.14, W. INF. BDE. "B" Company attached to 6 & 7 2nd LONDONS by Platoon. Left LES BREBIS – LOOS SECTOR at 4.30 pm. While A-D Coys were forming up in the Church Square LES BREBIS prior to marching into their billets at S MAROC they were shelled by the Germans. The men's behaviour was 10th British. There was attached (copy attached) and earned the following Congratulations from the Brigadier Commander. 140th INF BDE 16th BRITISH their Coys attached (copy attached) A.T.D Coys moved off at 4.45 pm then up to CAUCHIES (dismoded) all front 4 Company, C Company was sent into the MAROC SECTOR with 17th & 18th LONDONS. All arrangements worked well and there was no further Casualties during this relief. The behaviour of all ranks was excellent.	
S.MAROC	17.1.16		No Chance of attachment. Two Companies in reserve finishing working parties in R.E. New came to settle into their new life well and did not appear to mind the shelling often wilts. S.MAROC shelled by the Germans.	
LOOS SECTOR	17.1.16	7pm	Two platoons returning were relieved by platoons in reserve. Reports from London Regt – good.	
MAROC SECTOR	17.1.16		Well behaved and actions satisfactory. This should have been some shell – men not –	

Army Form C. 2118

WAR DIARY
or
INTELLIGENCE SUMMARY.
(Erase heading not required.)

Instructions regarding War Diaries and Intelligence Summaries are contained in F.S. Regs., Part II. and the Staff Manual respectively. Title pages will be prepared in manuscript.

Place	Date	Hour	Summary of Events and Information	Remarks and references to Appendices
S. MAROC	18.1.16		The day – No fatigue parties furnished owing to relief to be carried out at night. Enemy shells on S.MAROC at intervals. Men funable to light fires owing to having only stoves in the cellars near their new billets.	
		7.pm.	Following relief successfully carried out:– A Coy relieved "B" Coy in LOOS Sector by 8th & 15th LONDONS. D " " C " " " " 17th & 18th LONDONS	
LOOS	18.1.16		1 man "B" Company wounded by sniper at night. A Company (Canadetta) reported in the South Craters. Reports from Canadian Commanders relieving Companies that the men behaved very well under fire and Lewis gun fire abt 6pm. Working parties found for R.E. after dark. Reign of Crestmoney attempt shelling took place at S. MAROC. Bombing carry food well	
S.MAROC LOOS	19.1.16	Day	No fatigues owing to the 2 Companies in S.MAROC being inspected & carrying Communication Lectures. The various billets nominally inspected.	
do	20.1.16		Nothing unusual happened in Reserve billets B Coy relieved A Coy in MAROC sector by 5, 14, 22nd, 23rd LONDONS D Coy relieved C Coy in LOOS sector " " " " "	
		7pm	Nothing to report. Stretcher bearers supporting Communication cut wire carried out successfully. The following relief carried out:–	
do	21.1.16		During the night 2 men C Coy volunteered for a patrol and did good work. A Lt & Platoon by Companies in firing line & Supports. S.MAROC more heavily shelled than usual – many Stretcher shells did not explode. The Customary patrols for R.E. 1152nd Div. New Bde Br. Brena.	
do	22.1.16	7pm	Fatigue found for R.E. A Coy relieved by B Coy in MAROC sector by 17 LONDONS D " " " C " " " in LOOS sector by 5th & 22nd & 23rd LONDONS	
do	23.1.16		Water supply in S.MAROC was cut off by the German shells and water had to be brought up from LES BREBIS.	
do	24.1.16		Fatigue found for R.E.– Day passed as usual – nothing worthy of special note. Whole Battalion moved out to LES BREBIS into billets. The relief was well carried out and the men no casualties – during the whole period of attachment the behaviour of the men under trying and most uncomfortable conditions worked well.	
LES BREBIS	25.1.16		Favourably commented on and all the staff employments	
"	26.1.16		Day spent in billets and cleaning up after the trenches. Battn Wagon moved into the Chateau occupied before by 141st INF BDE. Day spent resting and generally polishing up. Band inspected. Mass for men in Church. Orders received to move to back billets.	

#353 Wt. W2544/1454 700,000 5/15 D. D. & L. A.D.S.S./Forms/C. 2118.

Army Form C. 211

WAR DIARY
or
INTELLIGENCE SUMMARY.
(Erase heading not required.)

Instructions regarding War Diaries and Intelligence Summaries are contained in F.S. Regs., Part II. and the Staff Manual respectively. Title pages will be prepared in manuscript.

Place	Date	Hour	Summary of Events and Information	Remarks and references to Appendices
LES BREBIS	27.1.16	10.30am	Left LES BREBIS by Platoons at 200 yards interval for safety. Route via PETIT SAINS - NOEUX-LES-MINES to MARLES-LES-MINES (FRANCE LENS II G.1. $\frac{1}{100,000}$). Men marched light - Company mechanical Corps motor lorries provided for transport of packs, blankets re Brunis with fuel - Bt. Gen. THWAITES watched the Battalion march from LES BREBIS & expressed his final satisfaction at the workmanlike bearing & attachment. Cmdg 147th INF BDE	
NOEUX-LES-MINES	27.1.16	11.30am	Closed up the Battalion onto Column of Route - met from the Brigadier General Cmdg 147 INF BDE.	
MARLES-LES-MINES	"	5.30pm	Arrived and settled into billets - Arrangements good.	
do	28.1.16	10.a.m	Marched out from MARLES-LES-MINES and marched via AUCHEL - FERFAY - AMETTES - FONTAINES-LES-HERMANS to LIVOSSART and PALFART (Map: FRANCE. HAZEBROUCK. D.6 TOWN) where we billeted - arriving 5.10 pm. At AMETTES the G.O.C 16th DIVISION saw the men on the march and complimented them on their marching. Same Arrangements made for carrying packs, blankets - Billets C & D Companies at PALFART. A & B HQrs at LIVOSSART good.	
LIVOSSART & PALFART	29.1.16		Settling into billets - Parade cleaning up the billets, billet areas and dirty - breeding accumulation - no parade this day - Men very cheery & fit.	
do	30.1.16	—	A Company sent to AIRES to provide fatigues for 16th Div'l Bombing School. Inspection by Midmont Cmnd at 9.30 am for squad drill musketry - Captain paraded at 9 a.m. for squad Drill manual Parade hrs 9 - 12.30 and 2 - 4.30 cancelled	
do	31.1.16	—	Battalion parties carried out Bouries, Machine Gunner, Signal Training duties mett from D.O.B	
do	1.2.16	—	Visit from L/D6 16th DIV and 2nd Lt. 47th INF BDE	

G.O. in Bartley Lt. Colonel
Cmd 7th [illegible]

Copy of letter from GOC 141st INF BDE
to Major General Commanding
47th DIVISION.

I wish to bring to the notice of the
Major General Commanding the following
incident:-

While two Companies of the 7th LEINSTER
REGT were assembling in the Church Square
at LES BREBIS preparatory to going into
their billets at S. MAROC they came under
fire from 88 Shells (there were 10 Casualties)
The behaviour of the men was excellent.
They showed Considerable Coolness under
fire and marched off up to time
and in good order.

Signed Brig Gen THWAITES.
17/1/16. Commanding 141st INF BDE.

16 DIV
47 BDE

7th Bn Leinster Regt.
~~Nov 1917~~
1917 Nov & Dec

Box 1682

BATTLEDRESS QUESTIONNAIRE

Confidential

War Diary
of
7th S. Bn. The Leinster Regt
4th Corps
From 4th February to 29th February 1916

Volume II

Army Form C.2118.

WAR DIARY
or
INTELLIGENCE SUMMARY.
(Erase heading not required.)

7th LEINSTER REGT.

Place	Date	Hour	Summary of Events and Information	Remarks and references to Appendices
PACFART LIVOSSART A.13.b.36.B.	4.2.16		Orders received to move to trenches. Work in willows. A Coy. relieved by "C" Coy at LAIRES. 16th DIV. School. Signal Drill - Bayonet fighting etc.	
do	5.2.16		Routine work in willows. Visit from Brigadier.	
do	6.2.16	12 Noon	Batt. less "C" Company marched to NEDON and NEDONCHELLE en route for BETHUNE. Rainy. Very wet march. No lorries provided - men heavily equipped.	
NEDON & NEDONCHELLE		3 pm	Arrived NEDON NEDONCHELLE. Get-led into willows huts. C-D Coys at NEDONCHELLE. A-B Coys Transport at NEDON. Rain heavy - men very wet. C Coys Billets recent.	
do	7.2.16		Companies working independently - musketry squad drill re inspected by Brigadier who was very pleased with work done.	
		11.30 am	C Company arrived from LAIRES and joined the Battalion. Arrived near day. Orders received to proceed to MARLES-LES-MINES instead of LILLERS on 8.2.16 to billet for night.	
do	8.2.16	10 am	Marched out en route for MARLES-MINES. Lorries provided for Batt. CO + Adjt went forward to 33rd DIV by motor Car to BETHUNE to make arrangements for attachment for to 33rd DIV. 2nd in Comm and took Batt. to MARLES-LES-MINES. Fine day - men in good spirits. Capt PHILLIPS acting Adjt.	
MARLES-LES-MINES		3.30 pm	Arrived MARLES-LES-MINES. Same billets taken up as on previous stay. Mess. everything running smoothly.	
		8 pm	CO + Adjt returned	
do	9.2.16	10 am	Marched out for BETHUNE. Motor despatch rider attacked from Div H.Q.	
BETHUNE.		4 pm	Arrived in BETHUNE. Transport going by different route to avoid hill. Came under orders f 33rd DIV. Company office. A/s orders recd. no. 10-2.16. 2 Coys billetted Ecore de JEUNES FILLES - 2 Coys at FERNIE DU ROI. went forward to be round the trenches near Cuinchy on 10.2.	

2353 Wt. W2514/1454 700,000 5/15 D. D. & L. A.D.S.S./Forms/C.2118.

Army Form C. 2118.

WAR DIARY
or
INTELLIGENCE SUMMARY.   7th LEINSTER REGT
(Erase heading not required.)

Instructions regarding War Diaries and Intelligence Summaries are contained in F. S. Regs., Part II. and the Staff Manual respectively. Title pages will be prepared in manuscript.

Place	Date	Hour	Summary of Events and Information	Remarks and references to Appendices
BETHUNE	10.2.16		Day spent upon parties for Companies before into trenches in attachment at night	
ANNEQUIN	11.2.16			
LA BASSÉE	12.2.16		Battalion went into trenches at night attached as follows:—	
			A to 20th ROYAL FUSRs ⎫ 98th INF BDE	
			B to 19th " ⎬	
			C to 1st CAMERONIANS ⎫ 19th INF BDE	
			D to 5th SCOTTISH RIFLES ⎭	
			The men as well reported on by CO's. Artillery fairly active and Batteries formed with 4 Coy. Many snipers. Enemy also feint snipers. H. Reeve wounded with A Coy.	
BETHUNE	13.2.16		Co. Offr. Grenade Officer, M.G.O. Signaling Offr / Company Commanders visit the trenches. W.O. who was the Battalion was taking us a spell in Clay Renemen that mortar to having baths at 33rd Div. baths	
CAMBRIN	14.2.16	6pm	Relief commenced. the 15th ROYAL FUSILIERS with H.O. Relf Coy ates at 8.15 pm. H.Q. Details went into trenches. Relief in the afternoon. No casualties and M.G. Details.	
do	15.2.16		Snipers + Enemy also M.G's active - Artillery normal. No casualties.	
do	16.2.16		Snipers + enemy active. 3 men wounded - 1 with wounds. Patrol event at night - also wiring parties. Much foot work done in Cleaning trenches. Visit from B.C.O. + 33rd Divison + B.M. 19th INF BDE	
do	17.2.16		Greatly increased activity in both sides. Snipe active and rifle grenades. 3 men wounded by rifle grenade. Enemy support. Trench Mortars very active in bullet + shrapnel shells on front. Much damage done visit from Brigadier trenches. Hourly shell detail was received in the afternoon. The 15th [R.F.] + the 18th + 19th = BDE Battn. Commenced at 6.30 pm. The Reef later arriving about 1 a.m. with 18.	
			Battn. Commenced at 8.40 pm. arrived at 1 a.m. on 18.	
NEDON	18.2.16		BETHUNE men were safely feed - Excellent report.	
NEDONCHELLE			Marched to NEDON, NEDON, CHELLE. Commencing 10 a.m. and arriving at 8.30 p.m. With the Regiment the march was very hard in all kinds as they had very bad came and trenches the previous night - march approx. 14 miles.	
LIVOSSART	19.2.16		Continued our march to LIVOSSART - DAXFART and MONT CORNET. To our old billets.	
DAXFART MONT CORNET			Raining - men very lame + weary.	

Army Form C. 2118.

WAR DIARY
or
INTELLIGENCE SUMMARY.
(Erase heading not required.)

7th LEINSTER REGT.

Place	Date	Hour	Summary of Events and Information	Remarks and references to Appendices
LIVOSSART PALEART MONT CORNET	19.2.16		Settling into Billets - day spent resting - Cleaning Clothing &c	
do	20.2.16		Took under Company arms' events - Visit from Brigadier	
do	21.2.16		Inspected by Gen GOUGH Commanding 1st CORPS. Men marched well - no other work.	
do	22.2.16		A + B Coys bathing at BETHUNE C.R.D. Army mobility Squad's &c - Snow &c	
do	23.2.16		Companies inspected by Brigadier in Squad Drill. Lecture at R.Q Office by TRENTON A.V.C.	
do	24.2.16		Nothing worthy mention -	
do	25.2.16		Inspection of Brigade by Gen MONRO Commanding 1st ARMY, who was pleased with the men. He then went to the depot and marched by him in Column of Route.	
do	26.2.16		Routine work in Billets.	
do	27.2.16		do.	
do	28.2.16		do. Orders received to move to new billeting area	
do	29.2.16		Warm arrival. Packed ready for the move. C. & "A" Coys 8.30 am "B" Coy 8.45 am "D" marked off Starting point following order. B Coy 8.30 am. Marched inoff Brigade "A" 9 a.m. Column via WESTREHEM - AUCHY-AU-BOIS to NORRENTE - FONTE where we have lived up Companies with the last we have had.	
NORRENTE FONTE (1.35.b Sheet 35 A)		12.35pm	Arrived NORRENTE FONTE. Brigadier remarks on the march very satisfactory - billets found to be in a very dirty condition	

Lt Col Bernard R7
Comdg 7th Leinster Regt

Army Form C. 2118.

WAR DIARY
or
INTELLIGENCE SUMMARY.

(Erase heading not required.)

7th (S) Bn. LEINSTER REGT.

Place	Date	Hour	Summary of Events and Information	Remarks and references to Appendices
NORRENT-FONTES. (N 35b Sheet 36b)	1.3.16		Heavy snow. Work out of doors next to impossible. Very thorough billet inspection by Brigadier and C.O. Billets perfect good.	
	2.3.16		Snow very heavily still. Manual in billets as far as possible.	
	3.3.16		Snow - very little done out of doors as ground in bad state. A little bombing with live bombs and Musketry in temporary range. Gun return examined and no others issued.	
	4.3.16		Snow cleaning. Work in billets. Bayonet fighting. Musketry. Bombing &c. Pioneers new issue from Ration. 10ff/ex 160 O.R. draft from 6th CONNAUGHTS arrived and attached to no. until the return of their own unit from the Trenches.	
	5.3.16		Routine work in Billets. Church Parades. Concert in Divisional Canteen in evening.	
	6.3.16		Snow - little work out of doors.	
	7.3.16		Order received for move to new billeting area on 8.3.16. Preparations made.	
	8.3.16		Marched in Bde Route March to ALLOUAGNE - 7th LEINSTERS parade starting point Cross Roads (Sq. V.7.a.9.4) at 9.40 a.m. Good march - arrived in billets 12.30 p.m. Billets good.	
ALLOUAGNE (27a Sheet 36b/3)	9.3.16		Inspection of Billets - Routine work - visit from Brigadier.	
	10.3.16		Bombing - Musketry. Squad Drill. C. Coy sent for 1 month to 1st CORPS H.Q. on detachment. 1 Off. and 60 O.R. fatigue to FOSSE BRUAY.	
	11.3.16		Route march & routine work. Brigadier inspected Grenade throwing - was pleased.	
	12.3.16		CHURCH PARADES - Holiday.	
	13.3.16		Practised attack in 1st Bde Ground. G.O.C. too pleased. Maj. MONRO reprimanded - very fine day and men enjoyed the change from ordinary routine work very much. Afternoon - Lewis Coy Command.	
	14.3.16		Routine work. Supply - M.G. & Lewis MacBetty. Large fatigue party to ALLOUAGNE - BURBURE Rd.	
	15.3.16		Practised attack again. C.O. & Coy present. Routine work in afternoon.	
	16.3.16		Routine work in billets.	
	17.3.16		St PATRICK'S DAY. Whole holiday. Sports from 12-2 and 3-5. Men given an extra feed out of Bn funds. Shamrock (kindly sent by Mr JOHN REDMOND) distd & sports medals presented by Gen. BRACE. Posted to Company "B" Coy been filled to strength. Day very much enjoyed by all ranks. Fine warm day. Sergt. J. TIERNEY proceeded with D.C.M.	
	18.3.16		[illegible] Exceptional Bravery to CAMBRIN. Last week. 4th N. Coy sent to ANTI-GAS SCHOOL. HINGES - WEST SPAIRE G reserved in Manual of Exercise. Routine work in billets.	

WAR DIARY or INTELLIGENCE SUMMARY

(Erase heading not required.)

Army Form C. 2118.

7431 PM 1 LEINSTER REGT

Place	Date	Hour	Summary of Events and Information	Remarks and references to Appendices
ALLOUAGNE	19.3.16		Commanding Officer visited Reinforcement Works & Co. but also to Lecture over the line. 2/Lt O'SULLIVAN took over duty of Railway Transport Officer at VICTORIA STATION, LILLERS. PH & G SOPHE. No Routine Church Parade - Very excellent Zeppelin attack midnight passed over LILLERS - Bath Parade by CHURCH PARADE	
	20.3.16		Attack practised with morning - C & S present first improvement on last time. Bombing present using by MGs & Snipers. 2/Lt ROCHE & N.O.O.R. went to 47th T.M. BATTERY Routine work. Route march for 18 days 20ff 130R	
	21.3.16		2/Lt ROCHE T.M.S. attended to 2nd Army accommodation Return	
	22.3.16		Attack practice in morning. "C" Coy came back from 1st CORPS H.Q. having done excellent work there	
			Co.2 not proceeded - Adjt went to Ergoingue with CRE in French worker with Co. - very useful	
			work discussed - Public heavy snow 8off + 130R 47th T.M. Party attacked reconnaissance return	
	23.3.16		Advance Party went in motor lorries to the new Billets by M.G.O + Lieut Brenade at 1pm	
			Bn (PUTTS L.B/S Subsection) The Remainder being 10 officers (TM Party & N) Party M.G.O + Subn Majors 7off + 530R	
			Officer Sergeants, Snipers officer + Snipers, Signalling offcr, Signalling M(M) Party 10 Sgt Major & all sent to NOEUX-LES-MINES	
			Remainder of Bn in preparing to move up on 25/3/16. Billeting party went to NOEUX-LES-MINES	
	25.3.16	7 am	Bn KILLERS to ALLOUAGNE to KILLERS Station where they entrained for NOEUX-LES-MINES	
		8.15	Bn marched from ALLOUAGNE at NOEUX-LES-MINES at 11 am where the Bath went into Billets for 6 hours	
NOEUX-LES-MINES	6 pm		SCOTS met us and conducted us into PUTTS. The guide was somewhat late	
			Bn addressed Bn on Square prior to their marching to Trenches - Reached by Platoon at door returned	
			Companies Relieving 13th ROYAL SCOTS at CROSS ROADS, PHILOSOPHE at the points from 13th ROYAL	
			Companies were in and Relief completed by 2 am 26.3.16	
PUTTS & B/S	26.3.16		Trenches in wet condition - working done in DOZEN ALLEY + Trench line - Listeners instructed the	
			Latrines in wheat was just thick Enemy very retired. Very quiet from Lieut + 47th Suffolks	
			pleased with work done. Enemy Aby detailed over Support Line with Rifle Grenades - Bomb exploded	
			a mine in front of the Bath - When left dug out 5 minutes bullets sailing. Snipers were very active	
			Claims 3 kills and I am Grenadier with Rifle Grenades. In the early morning our LEWIS Guns got into a	
			German working party near BOIS HUGO. Claim 3 kills. Another Remainder on wire at night opened its	
			condition food Generally though old ruck in spots 10R wounded by Rifle Grenade	
do	27.3.16		Bn continued in trenches - Sunny day active - but yet Grenades and Aerial Torpedoes - we retaliated with	
			Rifle Grenades and Heavy Trench Mortar. Enemy shelled DOZEN ALLEY. Active Enemy sniping but Lieut Kerr's by our Trench Mortar	
			Battery. MGO + OR wounded on Artillery Battery observed their position by Lewis. M.G. position H 25 B.9.L. was fired	
			upon by our Trench Mortars. Small working party of Bois HUGO dispersed by our LEWIS GUNS.	

WAR DIARY or INTELLIGENCE SUMMARY

Army Form C. 2118.

7 (S)BN LEINSTER REGT.

Place	Date	Hour	Summary of Events and Information	Remarks and references to Appendices
PUITS 14 BIS	28.3.16	11.40 am	The enemy were very active in the day with HE Shells and rifle Grenades - did considerable damage. The enemy commenced to bombard POSEN ALLEY with H.E 4.2 HE and also heavy Shells. Very much damage done to trenches. POSEN ALLEY was blocked for about 40 yds and was lost. H.O.R killed 1 O.R wounded. Before our S.A.A Store in POSEN ALLEY and dug out it on fire. The burning of the S.A.A. blocked POSEN ALLEY except for about 6 hrs. Our heavy artillery was called upon and the enemy fire ceased at 12.10 p.m. Live mgs Cpl Mc Manus Communication system Company went to the breakers at 1 of our trench with two could be repaired about 3 hrs later. All messages were carried by runners round another way. There was frequently unfortunate as there were 4 Relief being carried out on Right and our ration parties exceeded in bring up rating at 6am. The enemy morning POSEN ALLEY was cleared and one found some of the light Bombstore which was near POSEN ALLEY was moved to a place of first safety as/o/49 Ammunition trenches that were carried in from Bde Amm Store and RE material from the CRUCIFIX LOOS Company rifle were Carried out of action. Is believed by D and A by Brown Reserve & Support respectively to firing line.	
	29.3.16		The day was quiet generally with intermittent Shellfire from enemy Infantry Support Line. Enemies Trenches - very little damage done. One O.R had no casualties Enfietton Comm Trench to POSEN HIFY was carried out and the firing line and was drained with new bricks Sta Section from R.E. Signal Communication trenches and there were renewed as that already lead. Order for our relief by 7th Royal INNISKILLING FUS remained late at night.	
	30.3.16		Quiet in the morning except rifle Grenades on Support Line doing no damage. About 9:45 the enemy shelled GUN ALLEY with HE Shrapnel doing little damage to our trenches. There was no casualties. Guides sent to CROSS ROADS PHILOSOPHE to conduct the advance party of 7th R. INNISKILLING FUSS to the various position in PUITS 14 BIS which they were to relieve. Leary fighting of the men Coys were the next day. Intermittent shelling with 4.2 about the evening by MG's relieved and marched into Billets at NOEUX-LES-MINES. Billeting party sent to NOEUX-LES-MINES to prepare for unit enemy out 31/3/16.	
	31.3.16	8.3am	HUGO LANE Shelled with heavy HE Shrapnel - very little damage done and no casualties. Sniper anyway with cattle.	
		9.30	CO & Coy Commanders Spralley Off Mustering Officer 17th R. INNISKILLING FUSRS arrived and were round our line to reconnoitre before relieving tonight. Enemy sending over plenty of Rifle Grenades supply stopped their fire. Communication trench were rear shelled with heavy Shells from about 12.30 - 2 pm on Supa claim or to PUITS 14 BIS. He was falling from the own works. It's own heavy fire to the German line to HE Ken Carrying Messages Guides sent to meet Advance Party of 7th R to HE CROSSROADS. Relief carried out successfully finishing at 1.40 a.m. 7.30 am. 1/4/16 - No O.R wounded. Marched to Zivell RENOEUX-LES MINES last Company arriving	

Jno Fitzsimmons Capt
7/R Leinster Regt

7th Leinsters
Vol 4

Army Form C. 2118.

WAR DIARY
or
INTELLIGENCE SUMMARY.
(Erase heading not required.)

7th LEINSTER REGT

XVI

Instructions regarding War Diaries and Intelligence Summaries are contained in F.S. Regs., Part II. and the Staff Manual respectively. Title pages will be prepared in manuscript.

Place	Date	Hour	Summary of Events and Information	Remarks and references to Appendices
NOEUX LES MINES	1.4.16		Battery into Billets and Casualty return after Steenwerk tour in trenches - no small parties in town. Major Amer. killed. Billets deloused.	
"	2.4.16		150 men from DLI's + 47 P. Fus. Bn. Major Monro proceeded on leave.	
"	3.4.16		Col. Buckley returned from leave. Routine work in Billets. Bren's Alarm. Men turned out satisfactorily - groups missed - duly of extra interest.	
"	4.4.16		Parade in Billets. No extra duties.	
"	5.4.16		No Company inspected by CO as CO absent. Daily parties for fur men. Camp Commandant.	
"	6.4.16		Parade m.o. and us HULLUCH SECTOR being relieved by 49th INF BDE. 7th LEINSTERS to PHILOSOPHE WEST in Bns. billeted by platoons to billets there. Were talked to by men Major Caines NOEUX.	
PHILOSOPHE	7.4.16		A Repose - Left trenches parties sent up to the trenches daily - not enough men remaining to do any training.	
"	8.4.16		Combr. Group - did a little training	
"	9.4.16			
TENTH AVENUE	9.4.16		Relieved the 8th R MUNSTER FUSILIERS in Bde SUPPORT. Relief well carried out. This area no billets.	
"	10.4.16		A Gue chappelled the Trench. Amongst our men Kelly casualty reporting casualties O.R. 1 Killed D. Jennader.	
"	11.4.16		Repair. Dug too work while in Support and parties working from the Brigade a scout wounded withing	
			Casualties trench Rifle P. Rifle bay 3.o.R.	
		10.4.16	Killed 2 O.R. wounded 4 O.R.	
		11.4.16	NIL.	
	12.4.16			
LEFT SUBSECTOR HULLUCH	13.4.16		At 1.30 P.M. we relieved the 8th R. MUNSTER with the Left Subsector BUIKAH - The relief was noiseless and accompanied by 3.35 p.m. Major MONRO who had just left all 20 CRATERS and 773 represented formed hay depot a senior officer along who fought that the great value.	
			Casualties 1 O.R. killed 3 O.R. wounded.	
"	14.4.16		The enemy was very active opposite MUNSTER and TRALEE CRATERS with rifle grenades and accel Torpedoes. We lost 1 O.R. wounded - enemy snipers active - He was paid quietly.	
"	15.4.16		The usual sniping and rifle grenade activity. At 8.30 a.m. the enemy also two trench mines at the day to was heavy shellin of our trench line - Casualties heavy. Capt Mn had died from the daught ngs were unscathed except for one R.M. exchange rifle grenades wounded one always got happily. Casualties 4 O.R. wounded by rifle grenades	
"	16.4.16		Bob sides very active with rifle grenades and trench mortar support line now shelled with early morning stuffness within happening. The Casualties were 1 O.R. killed 6 O.R. wounded	
"	17.4.16		The enemy was very quiet during the day but made a strong bombing attack on the 8th R. MUNSTER TRALEE infront from line. They were driven out with heavy casualties. Put time trench mortars and those the enemy out of the Craters. We lost 2 O.R. 3 killed and 8 wounded. Remainder of the night passed very quietly.	

WAR DIARY
or
INTELLIGENCE SUMMARY

Army Form C. 2118.

7th LEINSTERS.

Place	Date	Hour	Summary of Events and Information	Remarks and references to Appendices
LEFT SUBSECTION HULLUCH	18.4.16		ADJT. returned from leave. There was the usual activity by both sides with rifle Grenades and Trench Mortars. Our working party was disposed by our Lewis Gun fire about 11.15 pm. The day passed quietly. Chaulte 5 O.R. wounded by Rifle Grenade. Snipe-line System.	
"	19.4.16		Very quiet day except that at 10.40 a.m. the enemy blew up the left branch of my mine shaft E1. Rolling to mention into him within the midshaft. He advanced party of 7th R. Irish Fusiliers entered to make a tour of the works. LOR-A. We relieved 7th LEINSTERS 20/4/16 Casualties 1 O.R. wounded with Rifle Grenade.	
"	20.4.16		Batt'n relieved by 7th ROYAL IRISH FUSILIERS. Guides met at PHILOSOPHE CROSS ROADS at 9.30 a.m. the Relief was carried out without mishap and was completed at 2.15 pm. The men were very tired after 8 days in the trenches line and marched into billets at MAZINGARBE	
MAZINGARBE	21.4.16		Arrived in billets at 5.30 p.m. and settled in.	
"	22.4.16		Days spent cleaning up after tour in Trenches, making and baking the man rest from 22.4.16	
"	23.4.16		CHURCH PARADES. In the afternoon the enemy shelled the ABBATOIR with 5.9 and 4.2 and who were relieved to hold no more damage was done. Very little damage was done.	
"	24.4.16		Routine work carried out — bombers and Snipers went practice inspected by 2/Lts and 2nd Regm. Det Affs on gun units the men inspected by 2/Lts NOEUX-LES-MINES Rivalry from Lieuts. PEREIRA, 70 men Roads and PETIT inspected the phone. Very heavy firing shells in MAZINGARBE Chaulty in CROSS Roads and PETIT	
"	25.4.16		Spring Road. Very little damage was done.	
"	26.4.16		Quiet day. Spent in routine work. Conference at 9ft. I.B. H.Q. at NOEUX LES MINES attended by COI. 2nd in Cmd. and POTTS. Work subject to Re-nie Day. In Thursday in very useful points were discussed.	
"	27.4.16	4.15 am	The enemy opened an artillery attack on PUITS 13 bis and 14 bis which OWN returned. On Trench was good Simultaneously the enemy opened an artificial bombardment on MAZINGARBE and the Trenches which destroyed 2 billy patches of the Re-shelling. Everybody died down up. Standing to await orders to move up as the enemy attacked behind his fo- remained so for the next 9½ day our guns up fl 50 after stage anything to give his gas Normal and again steady by to far prepared for him — Orders to be ready to assist at MAZINGARBE were Pts from the morning	
"	28.4.16		Day passed without incident — one Slight shelling of MAZINGARBE in the morning.	
PHILOSOPHE E.	29.4.16	10.30 pm	We relieved the 7th ROYAL IRISH RIFLES at PHILOSOPHE, EAST RESERVE with Reserve HQrs in Billets.	
RIGHT Subsection HULLUCH	30.4.16	4.30 pm	Section orders to relieve the 8th Bn R. INNIS KILLINGS in Right Subsection as they had suffered in Relief Commenced at 6.30 pm and went off successfully being another Bn. AT.T.K. in the morning. The Enemy Bn. Brig. Cmd. and infantry Brig. Cmd. as the Relief was complete by 10.30 pm. They open an Angelo gas attack & chlorine The Trenches were quite impregnated with gas. The Trenches were in an appalling state fm. the morning. We returned unit had not Rest rooms dang & away Wyzi Casualties. Suffered greatly except fr. The usual Artillery fire Chaulte the enemy was very busy working in front line during the night and was - 5 OR wounded 2/Lt J.A. HODGES. Chaulte his heard fm our Lewis Guns	

2353 Wt. W2544/1454 700,000 5/15 D.D.&L. A.D.S.S./Forms/C.2118.

XVI Vol 5 Army Form C. 2118.
7th LEINSTER REGT.

WAR DIARY
or
INTELLIGENCE SUMMARY.
(Erase heading not required.)

Place	Date	Hour	Summary of Events and Information	Remarks and references to Appendices
"RIGHT SUBS" WULLICH	1.5.16	9.a.5.am / 10.45 pm	Rifle Grenade activity at Stand To. Received 2-1 and silenced enemy fire. Our line from Right Company area shelled with H.E. ring-D/F/C placed T/line. Enemy seen many times along the day setup Nd-B/Tr-m. Attempted to sleep by day and active. Climbed at night with the wind with Rear of Corpls. Fire from gas ATTACK. Relay parties were out quietly. Relay ed and filwired. Also made arts on gas ATTACK Relay moving gradually carried away by no Coy, 3rd R. Mun: Fusiliers. 4 men near scene Special Tournmt. Left early deepening the front and widening.	
do	2.5.16		Beyond exchange Rifle Grenades and Trench Mortars. Enemy fairly quiet. 2 OR wounded. Naval exchange T.R.G's at morning Stand To.	
do	3.5.16		Enemy Guns.	
do	4.5.16	1.30 pm	Enemy shelled VENDIN ALLEY and our Support line with H.E. 2" to 8 minutes. Army asg and H.O. Damage thrs was to be repaired. Gas alarm (false) at night. Men & Batn Hd at alert (Rptn opp. No 14 lesined. 7.R. LEINSTERS to be relieved 4.5.16 by 7th R. MUN: Fus. Relief started to be at 7 pm. RUTOIRE ALLEY and 10th AVENUE at 2.30 pm Trmm. Advanced parties from 7th R.D. Rifles arrived 6 pm. The Trenches being handed quietly.	
do			Quiet morning – some shelling – Support line east BERRY LANE. Relieving party 1 OR wounded. Sent to Philosophie.	
PHILOSOPHE EAST	5.5.16		East at 7.30 pm. H.Q. Lubarbon. Casualties fully carried out + Completed 5.5 pm. Batn until DUROSCOPE. Bathed into Billets. General day.	
"	6.5.16		Shot in billets.	
"	7.5.16		At the FORSE Shot in billets.	
"	8.5.16			
"	9.5.16			
"	10.5.16		Little damage except to one or two houses that for divers this 8" Armour piercing shell fell very near pending little damage killed every day. Plan made to change the Brunt. Self Lt. Ed. Du. Cros joined for duty to & Adverse parties went up to Left ⅓ PITS 14 & 18/15 Columbia to take our line from 9th R. MUNSTER FUS.	
"	10.5.16		From NS 16. Guide, 1 Platoon asked for to be at & with NORTHERN UP and 10th AVENUE. Coy in reserve. No shelling during relief. Coy H. Luba aceton.	
LEFT ⅓ PITS 14 & 18/15	11.5.16	12.10 am	Rely with R MUNSTER FUSILIERS complete. & by in reserve.	
			D in Subs. B in Left front line. Own support line cleared. Equipment and ammunition altered.	
			Station. Night Quiet – every dropped some track morts into CHALK PIT doing no material damage.	
		2.45 am 3 am	Considerable movement noticed at the rear of PITS 14 & 15. Three Lestsetron Balloons were behind the German line. A hostile aeroplane was seen having one of our batteries fring during the might the enemy was working hard upon his rail in front of our Left Company also upon the front line.	
R.PITS No 8/12	12.5.16	9. pm	Trenches cleaned and deepened. Salvage of ammunition and equipment carried out. One Stokes Gun surprised a working party of the enemy in his front line.	

Army Form C. 2118

WAR DIARY
or
INTELLIGENCE SUMMARY.
(Erase heading not required.)

7th (S). BTN LEINSTER REGT.

Place	Date	Hour	Summary of Events and Information	Remarks and references to Appendices
	12.5.16	9.30 p.m.	The Enemy retaliated with HE and Shrapnel, rifle grenades and trench Mortars in our front line, we retaliated.	
		2.45 am	Firing ceased at 10.30 pm. Shrapnel over the ruins was effective and no further injury was noticed. Enemy were seen working upon their parapets and wire in front of BOIS. DE QUATORZE	
		7.15 M	Slight effect of Tear Shells which the Enemy had been using on our left. Casualties Lieut. H.K. Purdon wounded. 2 O.R. Killed 7 O.R. wounded.	
PUITS No 14 B 13	13.5.16		Troops rearranged. Received orders for Tunnel strappers shelter erected at junction of Boyau 93 and front line. Dug Outs constructed, and 150 yds of new R.G's. Superceded in front of Bay 7	
		6 P.M.	Enemy were heard working on the front line, the Enemy retaliated with R.G's and Tom & Torpedos without doing any damage	
		4 P.M. to 5 P.M.	Our Guns kept about 60 shells at POSEN SAP and CRATER making very heavy rifle firing & pouring the Bombardment the Machine Gun open fire	
		10. M	Three Grenades fell into BOYAU next on the left was blown in	
		8.30 M 9.30 M	Enemy Trench Mortars bombarded enemy support line at PUITS No 14 B 13. We did not reply. Considerable work was done during the night upon the enemy wire in front of Ballard cache. Particularly evident. Yah and YI2, and what their front looked like did not look so quiet. But that work had been done upon the German Second line in front of BOIS DE QUATORZE	
PUITS No14 B15	14.5.16		3 Front and Support lines Casualties. BOYAU 20 R repaired and cleared. Working party put up 70 yds of new wiring The Dug Outs carried.	
		8.30 P.M.	Enemy Septimores R.G's and trench Mortars on our troops and support lines without effect. Our guns retaliated and silenced them.	

Army Form 'C.' 2118.

WAR DIARY
or
INTELLIGENCE SUMMARY.
(Erase heading not required.)

7th D BTN LEINSTER REGT

Place	Date	Hour	Summary of Events and Information	Remarks and references to Appendices
PUITS No14 B15	14.5.16		Considerable trench mortar activity was observed at PUITS No14 B15. Our trench mortars were trying whom the guns and considerable damage had been done during the action of earth and material thrown in the enemy's direction by CHALK PT with HE doing no damage to our trenches. The Enemy returned their fire in neighbourhood of LEINST E POINT and in front of PUITS No B.18. The remainder apparently damaged and 3½ dug 4 out 1. V.18/1.	
PUITS No14 B15	15.5.16		Trench line retained undamaged during bombardment. Nil. Our guns in support fire and CORK TRENCH. Our 9 inch giving a hearty but with 2.50 yards of new wiring in front of left and centre companies and he gained breaks in old wire shelling on North side made parts active during the day. Enemy ditto during the day. Rifle grenade activity very slight. Rifle grenade exchanges were active with R.Gs against our heavy T.M. which were retaliated on considerable bombardment by causing considerable damage.	
PUITS No14 B15 LEFT SUB SECTION	16.5.16	9.15am	Fire from Vardy Subject Line and BOY 4 11 Claveches. Two guns up during the night our Serra guns 7 times and Stokes thrown 13 rounds at Volume. The enemy retaliated on CORK TRENCH and Reserve line with A.E. Shrapnel, no damage was about 50 C.P. of that shells failed to explode. Shelling continued until 9.45pm. One killed on the German trench.	
LEFT SUB SECTION	17.5.16		Very quiet day. Exchange of rifle Grenades. Relieved by 7th R Irish Rifles and 13th R.I. at Coy PT. DE QUATRE Relief carried out by daylight complete at 7.30pm. Guarallio one O.R. killed Coy PT. DUBLINS to relieved our Coy Co. Bn marched into Billets at NOEUX-LES-MINES.	
NOEUX LES MINES.	18.5.16 5 25.5.16		Routine work carried out in Billets. Special practice at night with a patrol party – very successful breaking train on Sunday and enemy shelled NOEUX-LES-MINES. One O.R. killed. Tours of the fathers arrived now Society besieged by Church Parade.	
PHILOSOPHE WEST	25.5.16		Relieved 8th DUBLINS in PHILOSOPHE WEST. Henry by firing into Myside Reserve. No working parties. Settled into Billets.	
	26.5.16	11 am	Working parties found for R.E. 20 and 200 O.R. Arrangements made for defence in case of Hostile attack.	

#353. Wt. W3544/1454. 700,000 5/15. D. D. & L. A.D.S.S./Forms/C. 2118.

WAR DIARY or INTELLIGENCE SUMMARY

Army Form C. 2118.

(Erase heading not required.)

7th (S) Bn LEINSTER REGT

Place	Date	Hour	Summary of Events and Information	Remarks and references to Appendices
PHILOSOPHE WEST	27.5.16		Routine in Billets. Deserter reported to Division on our left our anticipated attack in force on LOOS SALIENT. Large cloud of troops reported by Aeroplane behind the Enemys line - unusual Railway activity at PROVIN, MAZINGARBE, MEURCHIN. Orders received to reinforce the Bosche MAZINGARBE MINES if required. 10th AVENUE by 2 Coys. 5 Rifles Coys sent in to each Bn in front line as reinforcements. A & B Coys sent up at 2 p.m. arriving at 8.45. Enemy sent up by NORTHERN UP. C & D Coys warned to be ready to move at short notice - night passed quietly.	
"	28.5.16		Day spent in preparing preparation in case of attack. All fatigue parties cancelled. Church parades morning. Arrival two rations for Islands re. Day and night passed quietly.	
"	29.5.16		Orders received in the morning at 9.30am to relieve 1/2 8th R MUNSTER FUSILIERS in its LEFT SUBSECTION. Relief rather complicated owing to the unusual distribution of the troops. Grave annoyed and carried onto plans:-	
LEFT SUBSECTION		2 pm	C Coy moved in small parties by NORTHERN UP to relieve B in 10th AVENUE. B moved to RESERVE TRENCH to relieve 1/2 Coy of 6th Connaught HTS who were in majority garr MUNSTERS Hqs	
		3.30 pm	D Coy moved from PHILOSOPHE WEST and A + C from 10th AVENUE to the firing line relieving Coys of MUNSTERS sides	
		7.30pm	Relief complete - had were no Casualties. Me Coy of 6th R IRISH REGT came to Reserve Trench to reinforce our reserves	
LEFT SUBSECTION	30.5.16		Enemy working parties on front line and wiring parties out - attempted night. POSEN CRATER not affected. Owing to our having rather a line opposite the LOOP - with difficulty and our Stokes Guns fired 18 rounds on enemy front line opposite the LOOP - with difficulty for effect. Enemy fired with heart on KENDAL and POSEN HALLEY'S heavy bombardment with 8" and 5-9. In Reserve Trench from immediate opposite Cavalcade down due to the thanks me 8" didn't left. Bring in trench. Our heavy gun replied in POSEN CRATER and his Reserve and Emergency extn trenches. This was little on no Rifle Grenade activity reported every wire any army sling his front. Truck movement nia Transport betwix lines was put out V TEN DINLE & EGLISE CHURCH from at night. 2 B.R. wounded (Shell shock). Too + food wire four up during night.	
"	31.5.16		Very quiet day - no firing in enemy working party with Stokes guns + Machine guns as rest-dispersing them. The troops nightly were fed to	

Army Form C. 2118

WAR DIARY
or
INTELLIGENCE SUMMARY.
(Erase heading not required.)

Instructions regarding War Diaries and Intelligence Summaries are contained in F. S. Regs., Part II and the Staff Manual respectively. Title pages will be prepared in manuscript.

16 JUNE 7- LEINSTER REGT. Vol 6

Place	Date	Hour	Summary of Events and Information	Remarks and references to Appendices
LEFT SUB SECTION	1.6.16	12 Noon	Head Cover constructed at corner of POSEN ALLEY and support line where blown in. BOYEAU 65 and PAT TRENCH deepened, and wire put up between BOYEAUS 62, 63, 64, 65, 67 + 68. Morning quiet.	
			Enemy dropped few 4.2 shells on centre company support line, also at 6.30 p.m. trench bombthrown in in two places. Right Company active with R.G's. Enemy's retaliation with aerial torpedoes ineffective.	
		11.30 a.m	Our Artillery fired on enemy front + support line with shrapnel, and Stokes + Machine guns were very active, a German working party being dispersed.	
		7.30 p.m	Stokes guns blew up enemy bayonet + aerial torpedoes to route BOYEAU 67. Two torpedoes sent out at 10.0 p.m., one from BOYEAU 68 + reported to be working in front line + at mine between this front + POSEN CRATER. Although in enemy's front line two of Enemy appeared to be working in front line + at mine between this front + POSEN CRATER. Although in enemy's front line some of the slight wounds + sound of driving iron pickets behind chalk mounds were heard. Patrols came out of enemy trenches opposite BOYEAU 65. Much movement of heavy at trenches observed on line from METALLURGIQUE to mine buildings	
	2.6.16		Day quiet except for enemy firing few H.E into centre company support trench blown in in two places, and some sniping.	
		10.0 p.m	Enemy suddenly opened fire on right company front line with R.G's + aerial torpedoes and again at 11.0 p.m., to which we retaliated at stand to. During the night, 3 patrols were sent out and ascertained state of enemy wire.	
	3.6.16	9.15 a.m	Front + support lines of right + centre companies and POSEN ALLEY shelled by enemy; our artillery retaliated vigorously. Otherwise, day was quiet.	
		10.0 p.m	Patrol went out from BOYEAU 67. Enemy working party threw bomb at our party without result. Patrol returned to trenches.	
	4.6.16		Very little sniping + no R.G. or T.M. activity during day. At about 12.30 p.m. POSEN ALLEY was badly damaged at junction of RESERVE TRENCH by heavy shells.	
		11.7 h.m	Two parties went out with Bangalore torpedoes, one from head of BOYEAU 62, the other from head of BOYEAU 64. The party from BOYEAU 64 were nearly to fire at the other party were about 30 yds. short of German wire. The enemy had strong working parties on his wire and in front + support lines. At 12.55 our Artillery opened a heavy and accurate fire, the 9.15's also firing rapid. The face of the left torpedo failed about the centre of "no mans land" where it had been cut by shrapnel but the end was found + the torpedo exploded. Under cover of the Artillery fire, the right party took them torpedo forward at the double + placed it successfully and a third party placed and exploded a torpedo near pt. X 3 to the left. Party went about 6 fire steps. All parties were recalled through a signal mistake. The Germans had sent up a red light + shortly G.R. Leverage Capt. + Lt. Col. Commanding 7 Leinster Reg	

2353 Wt. W2544/7454 700,000 5/15 D, D, & L. A.B.S.S./Forms/C. 2118.

WAR DIARY
or
INTELLIGENCE SUMMARY.
(Erase heading not required.)

Army Form C. 2118.

Instructions regarding War Diaries and Intelligence Summaries are contained in F.S. Regs, Part II. and the Staff Manual respectively. Title pages will be prepared in manuscript.

Place	Date	Hour	Summary of Events and Information	Remarks and references to Appendices
LEFT SUB SECTION	5.6.16	3.0 p.m.	into gun and their artillery now opened into front and support lines and Boyaus, but with practically no effect. The right torpedo was exploded. All the torpedoes were effective and made good gaps in enemy wire. There was very little rifle fire from enemy trenches except towards the end and only on LOOP HEAD and no machine gun fire. Enemy very active with R.G.s and aerial torpedoes on right and centre companyfronts especially about LOOP HEAD. In retaliation 4 aerial torpedoes were fired at our front line about 60 N. of POSEN ALLEY. Our artillery opened occasional bursts of shrapnel on enemy front line and our heavy guns were active on the gaps, in the wire.	
		2.30 a.m.	Enemy bombardment on front + support lines with infrequent sniper shinned from hits, one we believe gutted who had been watched firing over hour	
	6.6.16		Between 3.30 p.m. + 5.30 p.m. + 6.15 p.m. + 9.10 p.m. enemy active with R.Gs, T.Ms + aerial Torpedoes on R.G.s + Stokes guns retaliated.	
		5.30 p.m.	Enemy shelled front of Boyaus by w.tt of infrequent 4.2 guns with gas. Our artilley searching for Stokes Guns. Only damaging trench. Our 2 infantry 18 pdrs retaliated. Enemy T.M. + our M.G.s + R.G.s + T.M.s Right of an intersmyeltat fire on infantrywork is retal. were still open. A Gun emplacement was observed at H 20 d 50.65, its gun pointing S.W.	
PUTTS 14 BIS	7.6.16		Front + Sup Dutch cleaned & repaired. Relief carried out. Fatigue parties supplied.	
BDE SUPPORT	8.6.16		2 hour exps made our company in reserve trench. No change done. Clearing of trenches proceeded with, + dugout as repairs parties supplied.	
	9.6.16		Working parties supplied. Work was proceeded with on dugout of sanitary at junction of GUN TRENCH + RAILWAY ALLEY started yesterday.	
	10.6.16		Work on dugout continued. Usual of considerable men on working parties. There was abnormal movement of troops along the BENIFONTAINE VENDIN LE VIEIL road particularly from BENIFONTAINE.	
MAZINGARBE	11.6.16 12.6.16 13.6.16 14.6.16 15.6.16 16.6.16 17.6.16		In billets. During day, when not furnishing working parties, carried out instruction & drill, & various inspections. Sunday working parties furnished at night.	
BDE SUPPORT	18.6.16		Nothing unusual occurred.	

G.R. Dancroft Capt for Lt Col
Commanding 7 Kings Lt Reg.

Army Form C. 2118

WAR DIARY
or
INTELLIGENCE SUMMARY.
(Erase heading not required.)

Place	Date	Hour	Summary of Events and Information	Remarks and references to Appendices
BRIGADE SUPPORT	14.6.16 / 21.6.16 / 22.6.16		Completed quiet. Working parties detailed for carrying up stores to front line & repairs to line where blown in.	
RIGHT SUB SECTION LOOS	22.6.16 / 23.6.16 / 24.6.16	6.30 pm Noon 3.30 pm	Enemy periodically active with 4.2 & rifle grenades. Intermittent trench mortar bombardment. During the day. Sap at head of left bombing post for about 6.30 pm. Morning comparatively quiet. Afternoon slightly active. At about 11.30 p.m. sap of HARTS CRATER was shot by our sentry and 2 stump fellers. Enemy got away. Slumping of wire. On their return fired 2 rifle grenades over dump of wire torpedoes into ROBROY & near HARTS CRATER. We replied with NEWTONS & STOKES FDNS.	
	25.6.16		During the morning and evening a considerable number of PIPES & NEWTON GRENADES in response to rifle grenades in the afternoon, but one was dropped in our lines & two also when ROYAL SUSSEX were being relieved by us. Our snipers were active and one by the enemy sniper, and he was very active with snipers.	
	26.6.16		There was no abnormal activity during the day. Arrangements were made to explode HARRISON'S & HART'S craters in conjunction with the explosion of 2 mines. Very heavy casualties were expected on the enemy as bombs were freely used in the digging of the sap and also in the search of the enemy party. Our artillery was active & M.G.s were placed opposite the enemy front line trenches to prevent & hinder him from removing. The scheme effected a stroke of reinforcements leading to obtain but was altogether taken by the advancement of mines & craft. We bombed freely, and apparently had motion to fear from their efforts, but direct observation was difficult. Our trench mortars attempted through the period from 5.30 PM to 6 PM to cut all enemy's front line defences, and with apparent success that days.	
			Between HARRISONS & HART'S Craters. All the defenders of these advance positions from HARTS CRATER were successfully bombed by that party, the Germans having been driven below to their dug-outs when the mines were used and our men were able to keep them for ten hours in their front line after the mines were exploded and blocked by bombs. After retiring to their own line — The raid was very effectively made by men of BANGALORE TORPEDOES communications was the end when machine gun fire was opened. One successful party got in at 11.30 a.m. with almost 100 H.E. shells with out trouble. Artillery fire stood fire & mill-opposed and there were three parties 6.2 Howrs, 5.9's and 4-8 of two field gun batteries engaged. No casualties but there were only a party of prisoners with those except we couldn't attack by a field. In no case was Soft brought back. The casualties inflicted on the enemy were very great indeed throughout the day. Scarcely a party of the the Subalts & front-line entrenchments was without casualties, yet their are no definition on unknown. Not attempted.	
BRIGADE SUPPORT	27.6.16 / 28.6.16 / 29.6.16 / 30.6.16		The artillery were desolated & the enemy active at night. Our Furneaulers were severly pounded back.	

EM Darrell/Major H.A.A.
Commanding 2/Leinster Regt.

WAR DIARY

7th (S) Bn The
Leinster Regt.

1st. July to 31st. July 1916.

VOLUME No. 8.

Army Form C. 2118.

7/LEINSTER REGT

WAR DIARY
INTELLIGENCE SUMMARY
(Erase heading not required.)

Instructions regarding War Diaries and Intelligence Summaries are contained in F. S. Regs., Part II. and the Staff Manual respectively. Title pages will be prepared in manuscript.

Place	Date	Hour	Summary of Events and Information	Remarks and references to Appendices
RIGHT SUBSECTION LOOS	1.7.16		Enemy activity with Trench Mortars during day, to which we retaliated with STOKES. Night was quiet	Casualties: 5 Wounded
	2.7.16		Trench Mortars & Rifle Grenades were again persistently sent over by the enemy, doing material damage to our front line trench. At about 9 p.m. enemy was again active: our artillery effectively retaliated. Our front and support trench suffered severely.	Casualties: 4 Killed, 12 Wounded
	3.7.16		A quieter day. Nothing unusual occurred. Working party at night cleared front line where blown in previous night.	Casualties: 2 Wounded
NOEUX-LES-MINES	4.7.16 5.7.16 6.7.16 7.7.16 8.7.16 9.7.16 10.7.16		In billets. Sundry working parties supplied at nights. Training & Manual carried out in daytime	
LEFT SUB SECTION PUITS 14 BIS	11.7.16		Carried out Relief in afternoon. At 7.45 p.m. enemy sent over what appeared to be three hours later aerial torpedoes which fell behind support trench between BOYAUS 63 & 64. One of our aeroplanes was patrolling during the night between midnight & 1 a.m. and enemy used his search lights vigorously. For channels his nose at intervals with LEWIS guns.	
	12.7.16		During whole day, Enemy was persistently sending over Aerial Torpedoes from direction of POZEN CRATER. Our artillery carried out 4 pre-arranged bursts of fire of half a minute duration, and the co-ordination between the various arms was very good. Enemy replied feebly with field guns.	Casualties: 3 Killed, 11 Wounded
	13.7.16	6.0 p.m.	Rifle grenade activity during the day on both sides, especially on front trench between BOYAUS 66 and 66. Enemy sent over Sundry Rifle grenades and Medium Trench Mortars on support trench, and salvos of pipsqueaks again at 10.30 p.m. on support trench near BOYAU 65. Night comparatively quiet.	Casualties: 3 Wounded
	14.7.16	6.34 p.m.	Intermittent activity on both sides during the day. Enemy opened fire with 4.2 H.E. Minis 3 Salvos. In retaliated strongly with 18 Howitzers & 4.5's. Enemy continued his fire, and we retaliated heavily, and enemy ceased fire at 7.2 p.m. Our trenches were somewhat blown in, especially near BOYAU 67. During the night our machine guns were active worrying enemy working parties & traversing.	Casualties: 1 Wounded
	15.7.16		Quiet morning. We moved into Brigade Reserve in afternoon.	
BRIGADE RESERVE PHILOSOPHE	16.7.16 17.7.16 18.7.16 19.7.16		Routine in billets. Various inspections, e.g. Iron Rations, Gas Helmets, carried out. Instruction & Manual during day. Each night provided working & carrying parties.	
LEFT SUBSECTION PUITS 14 BIS	20.7.16		Normal day. Some rifle grenade activity on both sides	Casualties: 1 Killed

2353 Wt. W3544/1454 700,000 5/15 D.D.&L. A.D.S.S./Forms/C. 2118.

Army Form C. 2118.

WAR DIARY
INTELLIGENCE SUMMARY
(Erase heading not required.)

7/LEINSTER REGT:

Instructions regarding War Diaries and Intelligence Summaries are contained in F.S. Regs., Part II. and the Staff Manual respectively. Title pages will be prepared in manuscript.

Place	Date	Hour	Summary of Events and Information	Remarks and references to Appendices
LEFT SUB SECTION PUITS 14 BIS	21.7.16		Hostile Minenwerfer exceptionally active throughout the day. At 9.0 a.m enemy was trying to locate our STOKES gun with Rifle Grenades & Whizz bangs.	
		10.30 a.m	Minenwerfer directed to FOREST TRENCH and MEATH TRENCH, to which we effectively replied with 19 rounds & a few 4.5s. Unusual activity by enemy again with Trench Mortars (Heavy) in about 150yds of front line french immediately to right of POSEN ALLEY. This activity lasted over an hour eventually being stopped by our 4.5s. Our 15 pounders seemed quite insufficient to deal with these hostile T.M's which undoubtedly have from concrete emplacements. The night was generally quiet. We sent out patrols, no enemy patrols were encountered. Casualties: 1 Wounded	
		5.10 p.m		
	22.7.16		The whole day was unusually quiet, and there was very little sign of life in enemy trenches. In conjunction with 8th Division arranged with Battalion on the right, we heavily bombarded enemy front and support lines with STOKES, Machine guns & Rifle fire. During the bombardment, enemy very lights were noticed to be wildly sent up from his support line. Casualties: 1 Wounded	
	23.7.16	11.30 p.m	Another quiet morning. Between 1 & 2 p.m. enemy sent over three shells near top of BROADWAY and all failed to burst. In afternoon our medium T.M.B fired a number of rounds on POSEN CRATER: enemy did not reply. The night was comparatively quiet, but he had a working party out in part of BOYAU 63. This we dispersed with machine gun fire and prevented from carrying out again. A strict observance was perpetually kept on gaps in the enemy's wire, and any attempt to repair same was prevented by us: arrangements were also made for these gaps to be marked up by boards in our own trenches. Casualties: Wounded	
	24.7.16		Morning quiet again. At about 1.30 p.m hostile MINENWERFER was in evidence, but was silenced by our T.M. Enemy sent over a number of aerial torpedos towards bomb of POSEN ALLEY and BOYAU 63, six in succession being dropped. From this hour for a space of 2 hours enemy was using his medium guns freely, these seemed to have been brought up during the day, as the previous day it had been noticed how quiet his machine guns were. Enemy appeared to be very wide awake, probably on account of the recent raids directed against him. not of night was usual.	
	25.7.16	9.30 p.m	All the morning was quiet on this sub section front. Early in the afternoon his medium T.M was firing on our front line. Our retaliation with STOKES (amongst some 4.7.2 from him) from METALLURGIQUE but these stopped immediately we put 15 rounds directed against him. Casualties: 2 Wounded	
		12.20 a.m	A small party of 1 officer and 10 O.R's left our trench at the boyhead with a BANGALORE TORPEDO. This was successful exploded but did not cut the enemy wire right through as the top of the parapet was moved. Each member of the party threw 2 bombs into enemy's trench and returned. On the explosion of the Torpedo, enemy stopped sniping and Machine Gun fire but our Rifle Grenades, but was silenced him with our Trench Mortars. During the night he sent over Rifle Grenades, but was silenced him with our Trench Mortars. Casualties: 1 Killed, 4 Wounded	
BRIGADE RESERVE PHILOSOPHE	26.7.16		In billets, after relief in the morning: furnished working & carrying parties.	
	27.7.16 28.7.16 29.7.16 30.7.16		In billets: usual training & inspections during the day: furnished working and carrying parties each night	
MAZINGARBE	31.7.16		Moved out of Brigade Reserve: settled in new billets.	

G R Leaveroff Capt & Adjt
7 Leinster Reg
Commanding

Vol 8

WAR DIARY.

7th Munster Regiment

MONTH OF AUGUST, 1916.

VOLUME :- 9

H.Q 47th Bde

Herewith War Diary from the 10th August – 31st Aug 1916.

The Officer who was keeping the War diary has unfortunately been killed & there is no evidence as to what took place between the 1st & the 9th Aug.

This is very much regretted.

23/9/16.

RW Gaye Major
Cmdg 7th Leinster Regt

Army Form C. 2118.

WAR DIARY
or
INTELLIGENCE SUMMARY.
(Erase heading not required.)

1st Leinster Regt.

Place	Date	Hour	Summary of Events and Information	Remarks and references to Appendices
Left Sub Sect. LOOS	10.8.16	11pm	A patrol of 1 officer & 1 N.C.O. went out at 11 pm to reconnoitre crater opposite B 9 and B 3. Crater appears to be unoccupied & to stand about 50 YDS clear of trench. Very strong enemy wire between them. Found that the lip of the crater & enemy had a strong working party on lip South of the crater & level with it. Patrol returned at 12 midnight.	
"		8.30pm	A small mine or camouflet went up near the slag heap but nothing unusual followed.	
	11.8.16		Nothing of importance occurred.	
"	12.8.16	10.30pm	An officer patrol went out from M.9.B. at 10.30pm and worked along right side of SEAFORTH CRATER to within 20 x of enemy's wire. The enemy wire appeared strong & work was proceeding on the enemy's trench.	
		6 A.M.	Enemy's Transport could be clearly heard. There is a suspected aerial Torpedo emplacement at H.31.d.1.2 & a running firs would appear to be firing from M.6.b.6.3.	
	13.8.16	9-12 mid-night	None of trenches on railway prolongation of Fosse 14 - Fosse 11 to the CRASSIER can be heard. But especially used for the carrying away of Rations. Our Snipers claimed to have hit 3 enemy parties. During the night the noise of German Transport could be heard. They apparently bring rations up the road to the railway at N.1.d.9.5 & then by trucks on the railway towards Fosse 11 at the LENS. There was some shouting that could	

Army Form C. 2118.

WAR DIARY
or
INTELLIGENCE SUMMARY.
(Erase heading not required.)

Instructions regarding War Diaries and Intelligence Summaries are contained in F. S. Regs., Part II. and the Staff Manual respectively. Title pages will be prepared in manuscript.

7th Leinster Regt

Place	Date	Hour	Summary of Events and Information	Remarks and references to Appendices
Brigade Support	14.8.16 to 15.8.16	12.30 pm	During our Trench Mortar activity left of the LOOS CRASSIER enemy let up 7 box kites & soon as our Trench Mortar activity ceased, kites were let down. There may be a common arrangement in these kites for spotting our Trench Mortar emplacements.	
		7 pm.	Movement was seen in left of Posts 14/5/6. Our artillery was informed & some 4.5's dropt near the spot. Trio of our shells were seen to fall on the Sap head at H31.b.10.45 much trouble is there being thrown up. Rainy weather prevents further observation. Constant movement noticed backwards & forwards between Points N.4 & P.3 and the usual horse at H.25.c.30.25. Possibly latter is a message station.	
Brigade Support	15.8.16 to 16.8.16	10 A.M.	On the 15th an enemy aeroplane dropped a bomb at corner of HUGO LANE. During the day the enemy's artillery & Trench Mortars were active against the southern & some 5.9's & Shrapnel were sent over into the village line at 5.30 p.m.	
"	16.8.16 — 17.8.16		Considerable movement in rest of HULL between H.31.c.1.5.9.0 & N.7.a.2.9. Enemy at work great attention to his wire & parapets at this place. Men constantly at work upon emplacement probably of M.G. at H.32.c.5.2. Occasional Movement in BOIS HUGO & behind BOIS RASE. Enemy working up to trenches in the former. There was a heavy preliminary bombardment by our artillery at 4 p.m. lasting till 4.45 pm followed by 10 9.2 shells. 5.9's being dropped & 77 mm were directed on the left of the LOOS CRASSIER. About 20 grenades were noticed in Bovine Trench but & allium water a salvo of shrapnel.	

Army Form C. 2118.

WAR DIARY
or
INTELLIGENCE SUMMARY.
(Erase heading not required.)

Instructions regarding War Diaries and Intelligence Summaries are contained in F. S. Regs., Part II. and the Staff Manual respectively. Title pages will be prepared in manuscript.

Place	Date	Hour	Summary of Events and Information	Remarks and references to Appendices
Brigade Support	16.8.16 to 17.8.16		The fatigues of 31st August were working during the day. This morning 17.3.16 at 4:30 am an enemy Aeroplane flew over our village lines & Lewis Guns made off quickly towards PROVIN in the approach of our machines.	4th Seaforth Regt.
LEFT SUB Section LOOS	18.8.16		Our Lewis Guns disposed in small working party during the night to the Right of SEAFORTH CRATER. Another working party was stationed behind GORDON CRATER. Our machine guns opened a few stray withdrawn to their trenches & were not seen again.	
"	19.8.16		At intervals from 7 AM to 11 AM a severe fire of Trench Mortars was directed on to our front line which was damaged in places. Our artillery retaliated & there fire was gradually mastered. At 4 pm, 5 pm & at 10 pm enemy opened a heavy bombardment with 5 heavy trench mortars between in company with fields guns & aerial torpedoes. At 9 pm his fire suddenly lifted to our support line & reserve lines, at the same time the enemy made a demonstration behind his own lines. The Smoke from the heavy trench mortars was very dense & observation was difficult. Our artillery replied but not until our Howitzers joined in so their fire Machen 300 rounds from heavy Trench Mortars were fired but our casualties were slight.	

Army Form C. 2118.

WAR DIARY
or
INTELLIGENCE SUMMARY.
(Erase heading not required.)

Place	Date	Hour	Summary of Events and Information	Remarks and references to Appendices
Left Sub Section LOOS.	20.5.16	Noon	A Patrol went out last night between B9/A17 4,3 & 4,4. The ground is very much shelled	4th Bn Worcester Regt
			up by yesterdays bombardment, but they found nothing of importance.	
			The enemy is quiet to day along the line opposite us	
			Transport was distinctly heard & groans by men of trenches at 12.5 AM in the LENS -	
			LA BASSEE RD.	
	21.5.16		Nothing of importance occurred.	
	22.8.16		" "	
	23.8.16		The Bn marched out of the line to HALLECOURT. CAPT E.L.L. ACTON rejoined the Bn at 9pm.	
	24.8.16		The Bn remained in billets at HALLECOURT. Captain ACTON assumed duties of adjutant	
	25.8.16		The Bn marched to FERFAY	
	26.8.16 }		Remained in billets.	
	27.8.16 }			
	28.8.16		Bn marched to CHOCQUES & entrained 2.1 pm for HEILLY	
	29.8.16		Bn arrived at HEILLY & marched into Bivouac at the SAND PIT arriving there at 6AM.	
	30.8.16		Remained in Bivouac at HEILLY	
	31.8.16		Marched to the CITADEL from where it marched into the Trenches N by W of GUILLEMONT	

WAR DIARY.

7th Leinster Regiment.

MONTH OF SEPTEMBER, 1916.

VOLUME :- 10

Army Form C.2118.

7th LEINSTER REGIMENT

WAR DIARY
or
INTELLIGENCE SUMMARY.
(Erase heading not required.)

Instructions regarding War Diaries and Intelligence Summaries are contained in F.S. Regs, Part II. and the Staff Manual respectively. Title pages will be prepared in manuscript.

Place	Date	Hour	Summary of Events and Information	Remarks and references to Appendices
In the field 	1st Sept		Battalion held line of trenches SOUTH by EAST of WATERLOT FARM. up to the WATERLOT FARM. GUILLEMONT ROAD.	
	2nd Sept		Nothing of importance occured on this date. Major J.R. Leonard reported Battalion remained in its composition but received orders for the attack on GUILLEMONT. on the 3rd September.	
			Following message received from 16th Divisional Commander:- "7th Leinsters The Divisional Commander sends his best wishes to the officers and men of the 47th Brigade and knows that their action to-morrow will go down to history." (Signed) W.H. Hickie. Major General.	
	3rd Sept		Battalion moved into its assembly trenches in the GRIDIRON at 4. A.M. in the following order. A and C. Companies in the front trench. "B and D." Companies in the rear trench. At 12 Noon the attack commenced and Battalion reached its first objective CROMPTON ROAD. with companies in close line in every	

T2134. Wt. W708—776. 500000. 4/15. Sir J.C. & S.

Army Form C.2118.

7th LEINSTER REGIMENT

WAR DIARY
or
INTELLIGENCE SUMMARY
(Erase heading not required.)

Instructions regarding War Diaries and Intelligence Summaries are contained in F.S. Regs., Part II. and the Staff Manual respectively. Title pages will be prepared in manuscript.

Place	Date	Hour	Summary of Events and Information	Remarks and references to Appendices
In the field	3rd Sept		been taken by surprise. At 12.40 p.m. it moved forward against its 2nd objective GREEN STREET which it also made good. The Borders did particularly good work by pushing forward through our own Barrage and clearing the village. They got as far as the CROSS ROADS EAST of JUILLEMONT and then fell back on the Battalion. Captain H.F. DOWNING was killed at about 1.15 p.m. on this day by Rifle fire. The Battalion held on to its position with comparable ease, the great difficulty was experienced in the evacuation of wounded during the advance. Officers wounded in this action: Lieuts. H.K. PURCELL, W.T. CULLEN, 2nd Lieut. W.A. LYON, N.H. UNDERWOOD, F.T. POTTER, H.M. HOLMES, O.A. FLYNN, J.J. HOLMES, R.J. FRANCIS, 2 Lieut. W. M°GOWAN the Battalion captured 4 Machine gun and 1 Trench Mortar, in addition to a quantity of other unspecified material. The Battalion remained in its position at JUILLEMONT.	
	4 Sept			
	5th Sept		The Battalion was relieved at 6 A.M. by the 7th ROYAL IRISH RIFLES and proceeded into bivouac at CARNOY and was complemented by the Brigadier commanding the 47th BRIGADE for its action at JUILLEMONT. Casualties during the action: 10 officers, 219 other ranks	

Army Form C. 2118.

7th LEINSTER REGIMENT

WAR DIARY
or
INTELLIGENCE SUMMARY
(Erase heading not required.)

Instructions regarding War Diaries and Intelligence Summaries are contained in F.S. Regs., Part II. and the Staff Manual respectively. Title pages will be prepared in manuscript.

Place	Date	Hour	Summary of Events and Information	Remarks and references to Appendices
In the field	6th Sept & 7th Sept		The Battalion remained in Bivouac. Very fine weather. LT COLONEL J.A.M. BUCKLEY went sick and was evacuated. Battalion moved to LA BRIQUERIE on the night of the 7th. MAJOR H.W. PAYE assumed Command of the Battalion.	
	8th Sept		The Battalion marched up into the line and during the night EAST of the Bemetz EAST of GUILLEMONT arriving in position at 10.30 P.M., and completed its task by 5 A.M. on the 9th. "B" Company was detached as Carrying Party. "D" Company was attached to the 11th HAMPSHIRES.	
	9th Sept		The Battalion this day was in Local Reserve. It left its assembly trenches at 4.45 P.M. and proceeded to take over the line held by the 8th ROYAL MUNSTER FUSILIERS in trenches EAST of the CROSS ROADS EAST of GUILLEMONT, which should have been vacated by the Battalion at that time. The 8th ROYAL MUNSTER FUSILIERS being unable to move, 7th LEINSTERS	

Army Form C.2118.

WAR DIARY
or
INTELLIGENCE SUMMARY
(Erase heading not required.)

7th LEINSTER REGIMENT

Place	Date	Hour	Summary of Events and Information	Remarks and references to Appendices
In the field	9th Sept		Our own and enemy artillery bombardment was intense. Joined them in the trenches from 4 & 5 P.M. on the 9th day and during greater part of following night. The advance was checked by heavy rifle and machine gun fire and the Battalion was unable to move. Battalion Head Quarters remained in position at Carnoy. "B" Company and detachment of CONNAUGHT RANGERS were brought up to the Cemetery at 2 P.M. Captains PURDOM and JOHNSTONE, LIEUTS. STUDHOLME and LAHEARNE were killed on this day. Also 2 LIEUTS. BLISS and OLIPHERT attached to the 6" ROYAL IRISH REGIMENT, and LIEUTS. H.A.H.BREN & T.W.FOLEY reported missing.	
	10th Sept	2.30 A.M.	Battalion was relieved by the 4th GRENADIER GUARDS and withdrew to Bivouac (Quebec, on the way by TROUES WOOD. A few Platoons (armed with machine guns) at the CRATERS, CARNOY, whence it set again at 3 P.M. for HAPPY VALLEY. 2 LIEUT. SMITH rejoined the Battalion at the CRATERS. 2 LIEUTS. MORAN and WHELAN joined at HAPPY VALLEY.	

Army Form C. 2118.

7th LEINSTER REGIMENT.

WAR DIARY
or
INTELLIGENCE SUMMARY
(Erase heading not required.)

Place	Date	Hour	Summary of Events and Information	Remarks and references to Appendices
Litherland	11 Sept		Battalion left at 4 p.m. for VAUX SUR SOMME, arriving there at 8 p.m.	
	12 Sept		Billets at VAUX.	
	13 "			
	14 "			
	15 "			
	16 "			
	17 Sept		Transport and Lewis guns proceeded to LA CHAUSSEE, leaving at 1.30 p.m. Captain J.R. LEACROFT returned from leave. Draft arrived (14 in number) 12 of whom had been wounded at GUILLEMONT.	
	18th Sept		The Brigade left VAUX at 10.15 a.m. Order of march, MUNSTERS, LEINSTERS CONNAUGHTS, ROYAL IRISH, and went by march route to 2 miles WEST of CORBIE, whence they went in buses to 4 miles SOUTH of ABBEVILLE. Battalion billeted the night as follows :— "A" and "B" Companies at	

Army Form C. 2.

7th LEINSTER REGIMENT

WAR DIARY
or
INTELLIGENCE SUMMARY
(Erase heading not required.)

Instructions regarding War Diaries and Intelligence Summaries are contained in F.S. Regs., Part II. and the Staff Manual respectively. Title pages will be prepared in manuscript.

Place	Date	Hour	Summary of Events and Information	Remarks and references to Appendices
In the field	18 Sept		LIMOCOURT. Headquarters GAUMONT. "E" and "D" Companies GAUMONT. Transport and Lewis gun Limbered up at GAUMONT. Captain GRAY reported from 1st Army School. Battalion marched out of VAUX on the 18th inst. 15 Officers and 289 other ranks.	
	19 Sept 20 Sept		Remained in billets at GAUMONT and LIMOCOURT, nothing of importance occurred. 2/Lieuts. C.H. MAGAH and W.H. COADE joined for duty on the 19th.	
	21 Sept		Entrained at ABBEYVILLE at 1.4 pm for BAILLEUL, arriving there at 9.10 pm and marched to billets about one mile WEST of BAILLEUL.	
	22 Sept 23 Sept		Took billets took rations. One draft of 17 men, most of whom had been slightly wounded at GUILLEMONT reported there arrival. Remained in billets, nothing of importance occurred. The following officers joined for duty, 2/Lieuts. W.G. REAGH, A.W. COOKE, R.A. DEMCH, C.E. DUGGAN and R.J. SHERIDAN.	

Army Form C. 2118.

WAR DIARY
or
INTELLIGENCE SUMMARY.
(Erase heading not required.)

2nd LEINSTER REGIMENT

Instructions regarding War Diaries and Intelligence Summaries are contained in F. S. Regs., Part II. and the Staff Manual respectively. Title pages will be prepared in manuscript.

Place	Date	Hour	Summary of Events and Information	Remarks and references to Appendices
In the field	24 Sept.		Moved at 8.10 A.M. to Camp 2,000 yds. NORTH of SCHERPENBERG, arriving at noon. A very stiff march on account of Lewis gun hand carts. 2 LIEUT. MAC. DERMOTT and one man went on leave for 10 days.	
	25 Sept		Nothing of importance occurred.	
	26 Sept.		2 LIEUT. F.G.O. MORPHY, J.K.B. BAYLEY. and E.D. SARLAND joined for duty. Draft of 14 men arrived.	
	27 Sept.		Battalion moved at 4.30 P.M. into new Camp at BUTTERFLY FARM. arriving there at 6.15 P.M. At about 6 P.M. a hostile observation balloon was observed approaching the Camp. It burst into flames about one mile SOUTH of the FARM. and fell to the ground. 2 LIEUT. W.A. LYON. returned from hospital and 2 LIEUT. K. BERNEY. reported his arrival. 2 LIEUT. SMITH. 1/4 Battalion for H.Q. ROYAL FLYING CORPS on attachment to that corps.	

T.J.134. Wt. W708—776. 500000. 4/15. Sir J. C. & S.

Army Form C. 2

WAR DIARY
or
INTELLIGENCE SUMMARY.
(Erase heading not required.)

Instructions regarding War Diaries and Intelligence Summaries are contained in F. S. Regs., Part II. and the Staff Manual respectively. Title pages will be prepared in manuscript.

Place	Date	Hour	Summary of Events and Information	Remarks and references to Appendices
In the field	28th Sept. 29th Sept.		Battalion remained in the trenches at BUTTERFLY FARM. Nothing of importance occurred on these dates.	
	30th Sept.		Draft of 30 men reported their arrival from the Base.	

M Graham Nevin Capt
Comdg 7th
Royal Irish Rifles

W A R   D I A R Y

MONTH   OF   OCTOBER,   1916.

VOLUME

7th Munster Regiment

7th LEINSTER REGT

Army Form C.2118.

WAR DIARY
or
INTELLIGENCE SUMMARY.
(Erase heading not required.)

649a

Place	Date month	Hour day	Summary of Events and Information	Remarks and references to Appendices
In the Field	Oct	1.	The following were awarded Military medals. 2107 Cpl H WOODS; 2595 Pte H KELLY; 2579 Cpl T.GOFF; 3187 Cpl J.H.MOORE; 2496 Pte T.QUINN; 3533 Pte P.BYRNE; 3353 Pte J MONTGOMERY; 3421 Pte H McGUIGAN all on the 27th Sept 1916.	
	Oct	2nd	Draft of 1 NCO & 6 men reported their arrival. The following were awarded parchment certificates. Lt Col G.A.M. BUCKLEY; Lt J.V. HOLLAND; Lt C.L.WATKINS R.A.M.C.; 3496 Sgt T DONOHUE; 4962 Sgt W KELLY; No 5533 L/Cpl A LEE; No 1629 Pte P MACBEDDY No 3533 Pte P.BYRNE; Capt T.O.PURDON; 2nd Lt E.H.DUCROS; 2342 a/c/m/s P CUNNINGHAM; No 2518 Sgt J. SHANNON; No 2735 Pte FRANKIN; No 6780 Pte A.M. KING	
	Oct	3rd	The Battalion remained in billets. Nothing of importance occurred.	
	Oct	4th	Weather bad. 2nd Lt T.G.O'SULLIVAN and 1 man proceeded on leave for 10 days.	
	Oct	5th	The Battalion relieved the 8th R. Munster Fusiliers & part of the 6th Connaught Rangers in the VIERSTRAAT sector. Relief commenced at 6 pm & was completed by 9 pm. Disposition after relief was as follows:- A & B Coys FRONT LINE. C Coy at SANDBAG VILLA. D Coy VAN KEEP. Bn H.Q. YORK HOUSE	
	Oct	6.	Weather fine, situation very quiet. At 2 pm the enemy shelled an enemy's redoubt known as the quadralateral & did considerable damage. The enemy retaliated with medium trench mortars but did no damage. Parchment certificates were distributed to the following. CAPTAIN E.L.L.ACTON; Lt V.J. FARRELL; 3321 Sgt D O'CALLAGHAN; 3178 Cpl DEMPSEY; 1967 Cpl D.J. HUGHES; 3421 Pte H McGUIGAN; 3353 Pte J. MONTGOMERY; 3428 Pte C.F. COOKE	
	Oct	7.	Situation quiet. Enemy rebuilt the quadralateral during the night & we shelled it again during the day with good results, & got	

Army Form C.2118.

WAR DIARY
or
INTELLIGENCE SUMMARY.
(Erase heading not required.)

Instructions regarding War Diaries and Intelligence Summaries are contained in F.S. Regs., Part II. and the Staff Manual respectively. Title pages will be prepared in manuscript.

6500

Place	Date	Hour	Summary of Events and Information	Remarks and references to Appendices
	Oct 8th		the usual retaliation in return but he did no damage. Casualties one man wounded on a working party.	
	Oct 8th		Situation quiet, nothing of importance to report. CAPTAIN E.L.L. ACTON & Lt V.J. FARRELL were awarded the Military Cross. 4962 Sgt M KELLY & 8533 L/Cpl A LEE the D.C.M. The following officers reported their arrival. Major T.R.A STANNUS, CAPTAIN G.A. READ; Capt F.L.F. DENEYS, Capt J.K. DICCAT and Lt J.M. CARLETON. Major H.W. GAYE assumed the Rank of temporary Lt Col & Major T.R.A STANNUS became 2nd in Command.	
	Oct 9th		Situation quiet. The Bn were relieved by the 6th R.Ir Regiment in front line & Supports. Relief took place at 6 p.m. & went into Bde Support. Disposition after relief as follows. A Coy & 2 Platoons of C Coy at SIEGE FARM. B Coy at KEMMEL D Coy at S.P.13 (men) & TURNERSTOWN LEFT & 2 PLATOONS of C Coy at FORT HALIFAX. BN HEADQUARTERS SIEGE FARM. 2nd Lt WELD & one man proceeded on leave.	
	Oct 10th		Nothing of importance occurred. Major J.D. JOHNSTONE & CAPTAIN J.A.J. FARRELL reported their arrival.	
	Oct 11th		Nothing of importance occurred. All men employed on fatigues & improving the lines. Weather fine. Draft of 11 men rejoined their arrival.	
	Oct 12th		Nothing of importance occurred. Weather fine but cold.	
	Oct 13th		The Bn was relieved at 6 p.m. at KEMMEL & SIEGE FARM by the 8th R. MUNSTER FUSILIERS. The Connaught RANGERS relieved SP13 (men) TURNERSTOWN LEFT & FORT HALIFAX. The Bn proceeded to camp at N6A in Divisional Reserve remaining there for 8 days.	
	Oct 14th–16th		Weather changeable. Usual programme of training carried on. Nothing of importance to report. Draft of 4 men arrived on the 15th inst.	

T2134. Wt. W708-776. 500000. 4/15. Sir J.C. & S.

Army Form C. 2118

WAR DIARY
or
INTELLIGENCE SUMMARY

7th LEINSTER REGT.

(Erase heading not required.)

Instructions regarding War Diaries and Intelligence Summaries are contained in F.S. Regs., Part II. and the Staff Manual respectively. Title Pages will be prepared in manuscript.

651a

Place	Date Month	Hour Date	Summary of Events and Information	Remarks and references to Appendices
In the Field.	Oct	17 & 18.	Weather bad, continual rain & showers of hail stones. Training as usual.	
	Oct	19 & 20	Nothing of importance to report. Weather fine. Very keen frost at night.	
	Oct	21.	The Bn relieved the 8th R. Munster Fusiliers in the VIERSTAAT SECTOR. Dispositions after relief as follows:- Bn H.Q. YORK HOUSE. C & D Companies in front line & Supports. A (-y SAND BAG VILLA. B (-y VAN KEEP. Relief commenced at 4.15 p.m. & was completed at 9 p.m. Third dangerous. Keen frost. Line was in rather a bad state owing to heavy rain. Nothing of importance to report.	
	Oct	22nd	Situation quiet. Sector has become a little more lively since our last tour. Captain F.I.F. DENEYS was slightly wound at 1 a.m. this morning.	
	Oct	23rd	Situation quiet. 2nd Lt C WEED reported his arrival from leave.	
	Oct	24th	Situation quiet. One man killed in action. Lt J H.M. STANIFORTH proceeded on leave.	
	Oct	25th	The Bn was relieved by the 6th R. Irish Regt at about 5 p.m. Dispositions after relief as follows: "B" (-y S.P.13 NEW & TURNERS TOWN LEFT. One Platoon of A (-y at FORT HALIFAX. C & A (-ys at KEMMEL. D (-y & H Q at SIEGE FARM. Relief completed about 8 p.m.	
	Oct	26th	A strong patrol of 1 Officer & 12 men were sent out with the object of capturing a prisoner & obtaining as much information as possible about the enemy's pn & line as possible. No hostile patrol was encountered & owing to the enemy's wire being very strong, the patrol were unable to enter his trenches. The men were unable to approach within 12 YDS of his parapet, the officer, 2nd Lt BAYLEY, getting to within 6 YDS. Valuable information was obtained. Further draft of 12 men reported their arrival.	
	Oct	27 & 28th	Nothing of importance occurred. Notification was received that Lt J W. HOLLAND had been attached the Victoria Cross	
	Oct	29th	The Bn. moved from Bde SUPPORT at SIEGE FARM to Bde RESERVE at BUTTERFLY FARM. The relief was completed by 1 p.m.	

1875 Wt. W593/326 1,000,000 4/15 J.B.C. & A. A.D.S.S./Forms/C. 2118.

WAR DIARY or INTELLIGENCE SUMMARY

7th LEINSTER REGT.

Army Form C. 2118

Place	Date	Hour	Summary of Events and Information	Remarks and references to Appendices
	Oct	29	Owing to a raid by the 48th & 49th Bde taking place at 5.45 pm that night - extremely important attempt at BUTTERFLY FARM - wet & muddy. 2.45 pm: Jo. B. O'HAGAN & 1 Cpl proceeded on leave.	
	Oct	30th	Remained in billets, nothing of importance occurred, at the usual fatigues. At 12 midnight a large fire broke out on the LA CLYTTE ROAD. 1st Battln. & 20 men were despatched to render assistance. This party returned at 4 A.M. having rendered all assistance in their power.	
	Oct	31st	Brigadier General PEREIRA cmdg 47th Inf Bde. addressed the Battalion at 4.10 pm & congratulated recipients of honours & parchment certificates.	

W Hay Lt Col
Cmdg. 7 Leinster Regt

WAR DIARY.

FOR

MONTH OF NOVEMBER, 1916.

VOLUME 12.

7th Leinster Regiment.

Army Form C. 2118.

WAR DIARY
or
INTELLIGENCE SUMMARY.
(Erase heading not required.)

7th Leinster Regt

Place	Date	Hour	Summary of Events and Information	Remarks and references to Appendices
In the Field D21	May 1	1	The Battalion remained at BUTTERFLY FARM in charge of improvements.	
	2		A bombardment occurred on enemy's right and left flanks & our guns on the right. At 6.30 p.m. on the 2nd at BUTTERFLY FARM. The Dublins & Brigaded Grenadiers attacked. Smith & Hickie gained the preceding up of a Turk	
	3		The Battalion remained at BUTTERFLY FARM. Most of the time men of fatigue	
	4		Day - no orders important Weather fine	
	5		The Battalion moved up to JOCK HOUSE, the road to CHOCOLATE BUTTERFLY FARM at 5 pm. Orders distributed as follows – Ranks & first line to lay opposite cmdt to lay VAN KEEP.	
	6		The 6th Regiment (7th Fusiliers) raided the enemy at 10.30 pm. The enemy fire. It was unsuccessful.	
	7		This morn at 5 am No. 4268 PTE CAWLEY, No 5092 PTE DONOVAN, and No 1912 PTE D WALSH, succeeded in bringing in a wounded MUNSTER from within 25 yds of the enemy trenches.	

T2134. Wt. W708—776. 500000. 4/15. Sir J. C. & S.

WAR DIARY
or
INTELLIGENCE SUMMARY.
(Erase heading not required.)

Army Form C. 2118.

Instructions regarding War Diaries and Intelligence Summaries are contained in F.S. Regs., Part II. and the Staff Manual respectively. Title pages will be prepared in manuscript.

Place	Date	Hour	Summary of Events and Information	Remarks and references to Appendices
St the free	Mar 8		The Battalion remained in the lines. Weather exceptionally dry. Enemy very quiet.	
	9		Quiet and no casualties occurred during this tour. The enemy aircraft were active this morning. 6 machines being seen.	
	10		Enemy aircraft again active, but the air superiority was in favor of ours. The Battn. was relieved by 4th & 6th ROYAL IRISH REGIMENT in the front line, we were places in Brigade support at SEIGE FARM. Casualties of casualties were:- "A" Coy SEIGE FARM, "B" Coy KEMMEL, 6 m. SPT & THE BELGIAN HILL. LEFT, MK 14 MEN of "C" Coy. 30 MEN of "D" Coy with 2 Officers FORT HALIFAX. "D" Coy KEMMEL, LIEUT J.B. JONES proceeded on 14 days leave.	
	11		Remained at SEIGE FARM nothing of importance occurred.	
	12		Remained at SEIGE FARM. 2/LIEUT J.O'DONAGHAN Welsh Regt for base.	
	13		1 Lance Corp. and Mr W.S.O. were attacked with SIO Discase, photo of RE until the wells handed finished.	
	14		The Battalion remained in Brigade support at SEIGE FARM.	

WAR DIARY
or
INTELLIGENCE SUMMARY.
(Erase heading not required.)

Army Form C. 2118.

Place	Date	Hour	Summary of Events and Information	Remarks and references to Appendices
St Hilaire	Nov 15		The Battalion reached billets by the 8th R.Y.L. MUNSTER FUSILIERS arriving in course of march at curragh camp.	
	16		The Battalion commenced training and the employ of men per company. Meetings of Huts & Lectures provided on to-day leave.	
	17		Notify of important occurrence from from companies.	
	18		The Battalion officers & N.C.O.s received instruction of organisation of transports. A draft of under officers & N.C.O.s arrived in the base. No 21516 L/Cpl EMYES reported to billeting officer.	
	19		Nothing of importance occurred at Brigade HQ camp with Corps Commander.	
	20		A draft of 100 men joined the reserve for the B.n.	
	21		Nothing of importance occurred in the day.	
	22		A draft consisting of four officers LIEUT FINCHELAND and 48 other ranks reported to the day bar, one came from the base. LIEUT SEFARRELL proceeded on to day bar. The Battalion relieved the 8th R.DUBLIN MUNSTER FUSILIERS in the front line trenches of the companies & each of Faulglenes, platoon & one's hip from linen 12 by VANKEEN and 80 by SANDLEY VILLA.	

WAR DIARY or INTELLIGENCE SUMMARY

Army Form C. 2118

Place	Date	Hour	Summary of Events and Information	Remarks and references to Appendices
B.H. June 1918	23		The line has been unchanged along our Unit frontage.	
	24		Much more active with his Lance Mortars. Our casualties being on an average	
	25		1 killed and 2 wounded.	
	26		The Battalion was relieved by the 6 Bn Royal Irish Regiment on night of 26/27 and taken over by 6 Bn Connaught Rangers, and went to Bayon Rouge near BUTTERFLY FARM. The enemy gave heavy shelling for some time but no casualties occurred.	
	27		The Battalion remained in BUTTERFLY FARM and was employed upon Corps and Divisional duties. Nothing of importance occurred. There was big aeronautic activity, two enemy aeroplanes having been observed flying at a great height over the Camp. At 9.45pm one LIGHT & HEAVY Bombs fell in the days(?) leave.	
	28			
	29		The Battalion relieved the 6 Bn Connaught Rangers at SEIGE FARM.	
	30		Disposition on completion of the reliefs as follows :— C and D Coys at KENNEL, B Coy SEIGE FARM and A Coy and 2 Coys at Home holding FORT HALIFAX and TURNERSTOWN LEFT at SEIGE FARM. Battalion headquarters at SEIGE FARM.	

M Crawford
Major Cmdg 7/Leinster Regt.

WAR DIARY FOR MONTH OF DECEMBER, 1916.

VOLUME 5

7th Leinster Regiment

Army Form C. 2118.

WAR DIARY
or
INTELLIGENCE SUMMARY.   7th LEINSTER Regt

(Erase heading not required.)

Place	Date	Hour	Summary of Events and Information	Remarks and references to Appendices
A.M. front	Dec 1		The Battalion remained in support at SEYE FARM. One Platoon of "A" Company on fatigue party of 180th Rens. I other Platoons refitting for the Base.	
	2		Heavy Rain prevented Refitment. Sick reported in during the same No 3318 L/C ANOTT, No 1005 L/C EDWARDS, No 10116 L/C ATROTT awarded Military Medal. No 7924 Pte BLACKBURN, No 5521 Pte COMPLEAR T and No 521 Pte MOORE B.	
	3			
	4		The Battalion was relieved by the 8th Royal Irish in the Henry Line at 6 a.m. & Coy proceeded to KEMMEL CHATEAU, the other companies in Clangheon Huts LIEUT COL. A W PAGE proceeded on 14 days leave	
	5		The Battalion headquarters and two companies were in the day in KEMMEL CHATEAU. At 10 p.m. the remainder of the Battalion with transport again regrouped. The Battalion is directed to proceed to camp of wooden Huts and Hutments. Much of the front held by the Battalion fell in others of come time.	
	6		The bombshell of ... generally had the enemy retrenched, he harassed most. At 1 p.m. instruction received that companies of BERRY HUTS close to DRANOUTRE on Brigade Reserve at 1.45 p.m. the Brigade having taken over the SPANBROEK SECTOR from the ULSTER DIVISION	
	7		Nothing of importance occurred. Battalion remained in shelters	

Army Form C 2118.

WAR DIARY
or
INTELLIGENCE SUMMARY.

(Erase heading not required.)

Place	Date	Hour	Summary of Events and Information	Remarks and references to Appendices
In the Field	Dec	8	A draft of 1 NCO arrived. 2/LIEUT J.C.D. WHELAN proceeded on leave.	
		9	A draft of 185 NCOs OR & men reported their arrival in the Base at Boulogne. Nothing of importance occurred.	
		10	2/LIEUT D.F. KEATING returned from leave. The following rank and file soldiers returned to duty. No 5331 Pte COLGAN, No 5137 Pte HOLLOWAY E, No 4818 Pte NOTT B, No 5371 Pte QUERAN J, No 5312 Pte WALSH B, No 5572 Pte DONOVAN P, No 4286 Pte MYLES C, No 3490 Pte HUGAN M, No 5285 Pte ELLIOTT J, No 2113 Pte McCOMISKEY J, No 5314 Pte HOLLAND E, No 2863 Pte CLARKE B, No 5173 Pte MURPHY P, No 5114 Pte MOORE B, No 2694 Pte ARMSTRONG J, No 4419 Pte DOOLAN J, No 1634 Pte McENCE W(1), No 5505 Pte McGUIRE H, No 5080 Pte BOYLAND, No 5310 Pte McCABE H, No 3234 Pte MORTON W, No 5354 Pte FORD J, No 5354 Pte MORGAN W.	
		11	Nothing of importance occurred.	
		12	The Battalion relieved the 1st Royal Munster Fusiliers in the left sub-sector of the SPANBROEK SECTOR. Disposition as follows:— "A" Coy (Chr cooker?) FRONT LINE and mounted officers. "B" Coy. S.P.?	

Army Form C. 2118.

WAR DIARY
or
INTELLIGENCE SUMMARY.
(Erase heading not required.)

Instructions regarding War Diaries and Intelligence Summaries are contained in F. S. Regs., Part II. and the Staff Manual respectively. Title pages will be prepared in manuscript.

Place	Date	Hour	Summary of Events and Information	Remarks and references to Appendices
In the field	Dec 12		B. Bn. FORT EDWARD held a PLATOON of 10 & 69	
			to Bn LURGAN CAMP, near BAROUETRE.	
	13		Nothing of importance to report. The following Officers returned on furlough:— CAPT IM JONES, LIEUT MALLON, 2 LIEUT C. WELD. NO 122897 DRIVER P, NO 4117 SGT SHIPLEY T, NO 3521 PTE LOUGHLIN T. NO 4412 PTE MULLEN T.	
	15		2 LIEUT BJ KEATING and another Officer on another errand under him were to do nothing except to look after the men of his platoon. This Officer was wanted in Command for that	
	16		The enemy then placed accurate fire of the Vickers Heavies at top of hill in the map following the fire of 207 & NEWRY BRIDGE marked for the valley we had taken. A burst of HARRY CROWE fire was seen to dislodge any of the men and a good number reported the issue. Nothing of importance to report day, very misty. About 4 his words.	
	17		CAPT. & ASSISTANT ELLACTON. Our 2 LIEUT SMITH M. reported to day. Barr. 2 onoff of 3.30 PM - raised high 3.60 M, made by midday. am	
	18		Nothing of importance. Barr 3.80 — Man reported the issue.	

Army Form C.2118.

WAR DIARY
or
INTELLIGENCE SUMMARY.

(Erase heading not required.)

Instructions regarding War Diaries and Intelligence Summaries are contained in F. S. Regs., Part II and the Staff Manual respectively. Title pages will be prepared in manuscript.

Place	Date	Hour	Summary of Events and Information	Remarks and references to Appendices
Lifford	Dec	20	The Battalion introduced by the 1st ROYAL MUNSTER FUSILIERS on relief in BILLSBOROUGH RESERVE at CURRAGH CAMP. The relief occurred during rising & was completed at 7.15 p.m.	
		21	Nothing of importance to report.	
		22	Coy of 32 O.R. name of Lieut Brown	
		23	[illegible] Coy Lieut [illegible] & [illegible] Lieut FARRELL J. MUSKETRY STAFF [illegible] LIEUTS. KEATING. 0/0/4343 INTER RUSTB No. 5234 Sgt REAHILL W to join 1st. Bn. FARRELL J.	
		24	CAPT. J. R. LEACROFT O.C. & LIEUT W. KEEAGH proceeded on two days leave.	
		25	Nothing of importance to report except a slight fall of Christmas half holiday manner	
		26	Nothing of importance to report.	
		27		
		28	The Battalion relieved the 1st ROYAL MUNSTER FUSILIERS. Relief taken up and was completed at 6.30 p.m. Disposition of companies following:-	
			"C" Coy SPOT LINE OUTER LINE OUTPOSTS	
			"D" Coy D.O.7	
			"B" Coy FORT EDWARD	
			"A" Coy LURGAN CAMP	
			2 KING OF MONTINEGRO the gratis appeared Cpl. W. Ring of BANVILLE, CLASS 4	

A5834 Wt.W4973/M687 750,000 8/16 D. D. & L. Ltd. Forms/C.2118/13.

WAR DIARY
or
INTELLIGENCE SUMMARY.

(Erase heading not required.)

Army Form C. 2118.

Place	Date	Hour	Summary of Events and Information	Remarks and references to Appendices
In the field	Dec 29		SPENT COL. H.W. GAYE. The Battalion paraded on the square & was inspected by the Corps Commander.	
	29		Both officers & men on leave.	
	30		LIEUT R.J. SHERIDAN proceeded on 10 day leave.	
	31		Now totally invaded by important ladies. The war years which ever may end of course bombed are illuminated in a confusion. The home we suffered seems to happen with attack on BUCKINGHAM PALACE on the morn. a meeting was from 11 P.M. to 1 A.M.	

W. Gayestil
Cmdg 7/Lancaster Regt.

WAR DIARY for month of JANUARY, 1917.

VOLUME 14

7th Btn Leinster Regiment

Vol 13

WAR DIARY
or
INTELLIGENCE SUMMARY.
(Erase heading not required.)

Army Form C. 2118

Place	Date	Hour	Summary of Events and Information	Remarks and references to Appendices
SPANBROEK SECTOR.	1-4	—	The Bn. remained in the line, nothing of importance occurred.	
DERRY HUTS	5th	—	Captain S.P.P. Alcorn returned from leave on 3rd inst. The Bn. was relieved in the line by the 1st Royal Munster Fusiliers & proceeded to Derry Huts in Brigade Reserve. 2nd Lieut. T. Donohue was attached to Military School for Gallantry at Guillemont. This officer is now with the 8th Border Regiment.	
	6th	—	Captain C.R. Pescroft returned from leave and Lt. Col. H.W. Cope proceeded to Army School for 5 days course.	
	9th	—	The enemy threw over some 4.2's & H.E. Shrapnel in the morning but without doing any damage. He was uncertain whether he was keeping us or on the 4.7 & 60pr munitions batteries 300 yds in rear.	
	10th	—	At 8.45am the enemy sent over H.E. Shrapnel badly wounding 1 man & killing a Cpl. The Bn. was then moved into the trenches of the Camp R. At 9.15am the enemy began to shell the batteries immediately in rear of Derry Huts and kept it up till 11am, sending over 35-7 shells in all but without doing any damage.	

Army Form C. 2118

WAR DIARY
or
INTELLIGENCE SUMMARY.
(Erase heading not required.)

Instructions regarding War Diaries and Intelligence Summaries are contained in F.S. Regs., Part II and the Staff Manual respectively. Title pages will be prepared in manuscript.

Place	Date	Hour	Summary of Events and Information	Remarks and references to Appendices
Derry Huts	10/4/17	At about 4/pm	Our observation balloons over Dranoutre was set on fire by an enemy aeroplane & brought down in flames. Its occupants escaping by their parachutes.	
		At the same time	the enemy started on the barrage again and dropped in a further 40 shells, several of which fell short, just escaping our huts. We had no casualties today.	
	11th		Enemy did not shell today & the day passed quietly.	
	12th		The day passed quietly. At 11-30 p.m. the enemy shelled the ravine to the North of us sending over about 20 shells.	
	13th		We relieved the Munster Fusiliers in the SPANBROEK SECTOR and took over as follows:—	
			A Coy — Front Line & Supports	
			B Coy in S.P.7.	
			D Coy FORT EDWARD. S.P.8 & Beehive Dugouts (2 Sections)	
			C Coy (less 2 sections) proceeded to Jung An Camp (remaining Coy)	
			To day was very wet & cold.	

A.834 Wt.W4973/M687 750,000 8/16 D. D. & L. Ltd. Forms/C.2118/13.

WAR DIARY
or
INTELLIGENCE SUMMARY
(Erase heading not required.)

Army Form C. 2118.

Place	Date	Hour	Summary of Events and Information	Remarks and references to Appendices
SPAM BROEK SECTOR.	14th	—	Nothing of importance occurred. Bn. worked hard on front line which was in a very bad state.	
	15th			
	16th		Bn. was complimented by the Brigadier for its work in the line.	
	17th		A & B Companies changed over. 9/ Snowed hard during the night of the 16/17th & most of 17th. The enemy is wonderfully quiet and hardly fire a shot. Nightly do we do some kind of repair. In the last 4 days we have had no casualties whatever.	
	17.20	—	Situation still remains very quiet. No casualties. Snow also lying 3 days deep.	
	21st		The Bn. was relieved by the 1st R.M.F's & proceeded to Curragh Camp. Enemy opened rifle, and artillery so to a heavy bombardment of 4.2 + 7.7 Ms on our line.	
	22		The Battalion remained at Curragh Camp in Dickebusch Reserve and carried out the usual training. Nothing of importance to report.	
	23			
	24			
	25		The Battalion relieved the 2 R.M.F's in the SPANBROEK SECTOR.	
	26		Dispositions on completion of relief being as follows	

Army Form C. 2118.

WAR DIARY
or
INTELLIGENCE SUMMARY
(Erase heading not required.)

Instructions regarding War Diaries and Intelligence Summaries are contained in F. S. Regs., Part II. and the Staff Manual respectively. Title Pages will be prepared in manuscript.

Place	Date	Hour	Summary of Events and Information	Remarks and references to Appendices
	26/1		D. Company - Front Line and Supports	
			C. Company - S.P.7	
			A. Company - FORT EMPRESS, S.P.8 and BEEHIVE DUGOUTS	
			B. Company - LUTETIA CAMP	
	27th		This being the Kaiser's birthday, there was a little increased artillery activity, but nothing of importance occurred.	
	28th		Nothing of importance occurred on this day. Enemy artillery much more active.	
	29th		The Battalion attacked the Front line here by 6th Royal Irish Regiment.	
			Distribution on completion of relief being as follows:-	
			D. Coy. - FRONT LINE & SUPPORTS — LEFT COMPANY.	
			A. Coy. - do. — CENTRE COMPANY.	
			B. Coy. - do. — RIGHT COMPANY.	
			C. Coy. - S.P.7.	
	30.		Battalion H.Q. remained at NIEUPORT DUGOUTS	
	31.		Beyond usual artillery activity, nothing of importance to report.	

M.J. Clery Lt.Col.
Cmdg. 7/ Leinster Regt.

In the field
1/2/17

WAR DIARY.

FOR MONTH OF FEBRUARY, 1917.

VOLUME 15

UNIT:- 7th Leinster Regiment.

Vol 14

WAR DIARY
or
INTELLIGENCE SUMMARY.
(Erase heading not required.)

Army Form C. 2118

Instructions regarding War Diaries and Intelligence Summaries are contained in F.S. Regs., Part II. and Staff Manual respectively. Title pages will be prepared in manuscript.

Place	Date	Hour	Summary of Events and Information	Remarks and references to Appendices
In the field		2	"D" Company, LAPUGNOY FARM and FORT MACATCHERMAN	
		3	The Battalion moved to the park, Coy in newly constructed huts Coys settling in from tents	
		4		
		5		
		6	The Battalion received a draft of 40 ORs from 4th Royal Munster Fusiliers	
			and Lieut. Col. J.F. Smith & 2nd Lieut. C.E. DUGGAN	
		7	2/Lieut. E. FARLAND returned from leave.	
		8	The Battalion remained in Rifles	
		9	Carried out usual training. Major A. LEWIS MD, CAPTAIN TW CARLETON & CAPTAIN JA REA proceed on 14 days leave in UK 9am	
		10	Nos. 25110 PTE GEORGE BURGESS & 4120 Pte T. HOGAN were awarded the Military Medal for gallantry in action on the morning of 14th November during raid	
		11	Battalion remained Divisional Reserve work continuing as usual	
		12	On return of men on leave to purpose	
		13		
		14	The Battalion relieved the 2/8 Royal Irish Fusiliers in the SPAN-BROEKMOLEN sector of the front line at 11.30pm. Relief was

A 5834 Wt.W4973/M687 750,000 8/16 D.D. & L. Ltd. Forms/C2118/13.

WAR DIARY
or
INTELLIGENCE SUMMARY.
(Erase heading not required.)

Army Form C. 2118.

Place	Date	Hour	Summary of Events and Information	Remarks and references to Appendices
In the field	Oct	14	"D" Company — Eden - Left Bn	
			C Company — Sop, SP8 and Piccadilly Support	
			A Company — Centre company, supports SP6	
			B Company — Right Company, supports SP9 and SP10 Supports	
	15		The Battalion remained in the ordinary communication for busy throughout	
	16		on same line as reported. Weather hilly and frosty. The enemy were	
	17		driven back to their old trenches and artillery activity on the part of the enemy been	
			for a long time accurate from many heights hoffman e-hanks not unusable about	
			by high forbm, shell, shrap of the time.	
	18		The Battalion was relieved by 1 Royal Munster Fusiliers in the	
			support line and went into Brigade Reserve. R.I.F we co-op'd relief begun	
			& reported complete by 11pm as follows —	
			"A" + "B" Companies - Kemmel Chateau	
			"C" and "D" Companies - Derry Huts.	
			Headquarters - Derry Huts.	
	19 20 21		The Battalion remained in Brigade Reserve during these three days. No much change could be done as when enemy's machinery employed in trenches. The men not on ordinary fatigues or training or a march or rest.	

Army Form C. 2118.

WAR DIARY
or
INTELLIGENCE SUMMARY.
(Erase heading not required.)

Instructions regarding War Diaries and Intelligence Summaries are contained in F.S. Regs., Part II. and the Staff Manual respectively. Title pages will be prepared in manuscript.

Place	Date	Hour	Summary of Events and Information	Remarks and references to Appendices
The Curragh	Feb 19		Battalion was divided into 2 Company Organisation. Owing to the proximity of Company Commanders in many cases not to Kennell	
	20			
	21		DEFENCES the work was curtailed.	
	22		The Battalion was relieved by the 3rd Royal Inniskilling Fusiliers and moved into Curragh Reserve. Disposition on completion of relief were as follows.	
			"A" & "B" Companies KEMMEL SHELTERS	
			"C" Company LONCASTER HUTS	
			"D" Company CURRAGH CAMP	
			Headquarters KEMMEL SHELTERS	
			LIEUT COLONEL W.H. GAYE proceeded on 21 day leave.	
	23		The Battalion remained in Divisional Reserve & carried on the usual	
	24		training.	
	25			
	26			
	27		The Battalion was inspected in uniform dress by the Officer Commanding the	
			47 Infantry Brigade, at Curragh Camp	
	28		Nothing of importance to report.	

T.R. Wilkinson
Lieut Col
Commanding 7 Leinsters

WAR   DIARY
FOR   MONTH   OF   MARCH, 1917.

VOLUME 16

UNIT:- 7th Btn Leinster Regiment.

WAR DIARY

INTELLIGENCE SUMMARY.

(Erase heading not required.)

1st LEINSTER REGT. Army Form C. 2118.

Instructions regarding War Diaries and Intelligence Summaries are contained in F.S. Regs., Part II. and the Staff Manual respectively. Title pages will be prepared in manuscript.

Place	Date	Hour	Summary of Events and Information	Remarks and references to Appendices
KEMMEL SHELTERS	1/3/17	—	The Bn remained in its present position. Nothing of importance occurred.	
DOCTORS HOUSE KEMMEL	2/3/17	—	The Battalion relieved the 7/8th R. Irish Fusiliers in Brigade support. The relief was completed by 4.30 pm. Distribution of the Bn as follows. A Coy. 4 Platoons LA POLKA FARM, FORT SNS CHIC HENUA being in a bad state of repair was impossible to put its garrison into it, it was, however, kept in readiness in case of emergency. B Coy. 2 Platoons FORT REGINA; 2 Platoons d/by H.Q. YOUNG ST DUGOUTS. C Coy. FORT EDWARD. D Coy. BEEHIVE DUGOUTS COOKER FARM CALVARY DUGOUTS.	
Bde Support	3–5/m/7	—	Bn remained in Bde Support. A very quiet period. Practically no hostile shell fire & enemy's trenches in places reported unoccupied & filled with mine. During this time the enemy flew a camouflet near Pickem.	
Right Sub Sec	6/3	—	The Bn relieved the 1st R. Munster Fusiliers in the Right Sub Section of the	

A5834 Wt. W4973/M687 750,000 8/16 D. D. & L. Ltd. Forms/C.2118/13.

WAR DIARY
INTELLIGENCE SUMMARY

7th LEINSTER

Army Form C. 2118.

Place	Date	Hour	Summary of Events and Information	Remarks and references to Appendices
	March 7		SPANBROEK SECTOR. Distribution as follows:- A Coy. Left of Front line & WISTON ROAD. B Coy. 2 Platoons HQ S.P.7. 2 Platoons Centre of Front line. D Coy. 2 Platoons Centre of Front line. 2 Platoons PICCADILLY DUGOUTS 1 Platoon S.P.8. S.P.6. C Coy. 2 Platoons Right of Front line. 2 Platoons SHAMUS DUGOUTS 2/Lt. W. CREAD was severely wounded in the morning of the 7th at 4am. & Died at 7am. It was buried that day at 5pm at POND FARM.	
	March 8th	At 3.30pm	the enemy opened a heavy bombardment on the whole of the Bn Front, that is from PICCADILLY on the NORTH to DURHAM ROAD on the SOUTH. SP6 & SP7 were also heavily shelled specially the latter. D Coy's front from REDAN AVENUE to BOWLES LANE was very heavily shelled that any other. The bombardment lasted till 6pm & then ceased but salvoes were fired every quarter of an hour till about 3am on the 9th. Captain G.A. READ was killed & this day. Total Casualty 1 officer (Captain Read) & 10 other ranks killed and 22 other ranks wounded. One of these had since died.	
	March 9th	At 4am	the enemy opened an intense bombardment on D Coy's Front & S.P.7.	

WAR DIARY

7th LEINSTER

Army Form C. 2118.

Place	Date	Hour	Summary of Events and Information	Remarks and references to Appendices
			At 4.22 A.M. the S.O.S signal was sent up from this Bn's Front & at 4.26 A.M. our artillery Barrage opened. At 5 pm everything was reported quiet. At no point did the enemy enter our trenches and our casualties were 1 man killed. The enemy left 8 killed in front of our wire and two unwounded prisoners in our hands, as well as lying dead in No Man's land he dealt with twice again & machine gun fire and as a very heavy barrage was laid on his front line he must have suffered considerable damage. The strength of the Raiding Party probably amounted to at least 100 men. Ourselves own dead were brought in at POND FARM at 5 pm and the 9th inst. Many telegrams of congratulation to the Bn were received from the Divisional & Army Commanders etc. 2nd Lts DENCH and BIRKLEY especially distinguished themselves during the attack and all ranks behaved with the greatest gallantry.	

Army Form C. 2118.

7th LEINSTER

WAR DIARY
or
INTELLIGENCE SUMMARY
(Erase heading not required.)

Instructions regarding War Diaries and Intelligence Summaries are contained in F.S. Regs., Part II. and the Staff Manual respectively. Title pages will be prepared in manuscript.

Place	Date	Hour	Summary of Events and Information	Remarks and references to Appendices
	March 10th		The Bn was relieved at 5.30 p.m. by the 1st R. Munster Fus. and proceeded to DERRY HUTS.	
KEMMEL CHATEAU	March 12th		The Bn was relieved by the 15th R. Irish Rifles of the 36th Division and proceeded into Back billets in the neighbourhood of FLETRE.	
	March 13th/14th		Lt Col J.C. DOBSON joined the Bn on the 13th inst & was posted to C. Coy. The Bn remained in Back billets enjoying a well deserved rest.	
FLETRE	March 15th		Bn Sports took place at ——. The meeting was highly successful and many events were hotly contested. Brig Genl PEREIRA commanding the Bde presented the prizes.	
	March 16th 17th 18th 19th		Nothing of interest occurred on these dates. The usual training being carried out. The New Form of attack being specially practised.	
	March 20th		Bde Sports took place in the neighbourhood of BERTHEN. It was a very bad day & in consequence the attendance was poor.	
	March 21st to March 30th		Usual Training was carried out at these dates. Three officers 2nd Lts BAARY & HAMILTON & DOBSON joined during this period of drafts. Amounting to 15 other ranks.	

A 3834. Wt. W4973/M68. 750,000 8/16 D.D. & L. Ltd. Forms/C.2118/13.

7th LEINSTER.

Army Form C. 21

WAR DIARY

or

~~INTELLIGENCE SUMMARY~~

(Erase heading not required.)

Place	Date	Hour	Summary of Events and Information	Remarks and references to Appendices
	March 31st		The Bn marched from its billets to CLARE CAMP en route for the line. It cleared SHAEXKEN at 10.55 AM arriving at CLARE CAMP at 12.15 pm. This was the first occasion on which CLARE CAMP was used by any troops. Weather fine but showery. The Battalion leaves for the line as Support Bn tomorrow.	

T.R.A.Mannus Lt Col.
1/4/17.
Comdg 7th Leinster Regt

WAR DIARY FOR MONTH OF APRIL, 1917.

VOLUME:- 14

UNIT:- 7th Leinster Regiment.

7th LEINSTER Army Form C. 2118.

WAR DIARY or INTELLIGENCE SUMMARY

Place	Date	Hour	Summary of Events and Information	Remarks and references to Appendices
	1917			
April 1st			The Bn moved from CLARE CAMP into Supports in the VIERSTRAAT SECTOR, relieving the 7th R. Inniskilling Fusiliers. Relief was reported complete at 1.35 pm & dispositions were as follows:—	
			A Coy. SIEGE FARM. B Coy. 3 Platoons ROSSIGNOL 1 Platoon FORT MOUNT ROYAL	
			C Coy. 3 Platoons LA POLKA FARM 1 Platoon SASCATCHEWAN	
			D Coy. 3 Platoons SANDBAG VILLA 1 Platoon FORT HALIFAX.	
			Bn. H.Q. ROSSIGNOL ESTAMINET	
			Relief was completed without molestation from the enemy in any shape or form.	
April 2nd & 3rd			C Company was shelled in LA POLKA. Casualties during these two days 9 men wounded. One of these men died in BAILLEUL on the 3rd inst.	
April 4th			The Bn relieved the R. Munster Fusiliers in the left sub-sector. Relief commenced at 7.30 pm and was reported complete at 10.15 pm.	
			Dispositions as follows:— A Coy Front line from the VIERSTRAAT Road to LARK & BANGOR. B Coy SP13 & VANKEEP. C Coy Supports. D Coy (less 1 platoon) Reserve. B Coy 1 Platoon at Bn. Butterfly Farm.	

WAR DIARY or INTELLIGENCE SUMMARY

Army Form C. 2118

7th LEINSTER

(Erase heading not required.)

Place	Date	Hour	Summary of Events and Information	Remarks and references to Appendices
	April 4th		The line is littler than previous, the worst part being on our Right where the 2nd Royal Irish Regt is. A gap of 300x - 400x between ourselves and the Right Battalion (Inniskilling 2nd Bn)	
	April 5th		At 8.45 pm the 6th R. Irish Regt raided the enemys trenches to their Front behind a creeping barrage. All was quiet at 10.30 pm. The raid is reported a success. During it, to screen our Front line, Support line, VAN KEEP and SP13 were subjected to a severe bombardment, the trenches especially in VAN KEEP being damaged. Our casualties were however very slight. 1 man killed and 6 wounded. (none slightly) including 2 shell shock. At 11pm the enemy blew a camouflet on the VIERSTRAAT ROAD opposite our Left. He was evidently very nervous and expected a general attack. The night passed quietly except for intermittent bursts of 4.2's in the neighbourhood of SP13, no damage being done.	
	April 6th: April 9th		The Bn remained in the front line, nothing of importance occurred, the enemy being very quiet.	

WAR DIARY
or
INTELLIGENCE SUMMARY.

(Erase heading not required.)

7th LEINSTER.

Army Form C. 2118

Place	Date	Hour	Summary of Events and Information	Remarks and references to Appendices
	April 10th to 14th		The Bn was relieved by the 1st R. MUNSTER FUSILIERS and proceeded into Bde Reserve at BUTTERFLY FARM (4th SE of G in SCHEERPENBERG Ref HAZEBROUCK 5A). While in Bde Reserve the Bn found working parties amounting to 220 daily. These parties were engaged on work on back lines, new trenches & gun pits). There appears to be great activity behind our lines.	
	April 15th		The Bn relieved the 1st R. MUNSTER FUSILIERS in the left subsector. Disposition as follows. B Coy Front line (from N.18.a.75.75 to N.18.c.4.0 Right Trench map W/TSCHAETE 28.SW2 edition 3.E). D Coy Supports. C Coy VAN KEEP and S.P. 13 & 1 Platoon A Coy 2 Platoon A Coy BUTTERFLY FARM. 1 Platoon A Coy FORT HALIFAX	
	April 17th		Two prisoners captured during the night of Apr 16th/17th by the 6th CONNAUGHT RANGERS, on our right reported that a raid was intended on that Bn's front & in consequence the whole	

Army Form C. 2118

WAR DIARY
or
INTELLIGENCE SUMMARY. 7th LEINSTER.
(Erase heading not required.)

Instructions regarding War Diaries and Intelligence Summaries are contained in F. S. Regs., Part II. and the Staff Manual respectively. Title pages will be prepared in manuscript.

Place	Date	Hour	Summary of Events and Information	Remarks and references to Appendices
	April 17th		of the PM was very much in the about, and the men there very anxious that the Raid would take place more fast	
	April 18th		The enemy remained quiet & put up a large number of verys LIGHTS. He appears to be holding his front line very strongly, but a patrol under 2nd Lt HAMILTON of B.Sy reported a certain amount of work going on in his front line.	
	April 19th		At 6 pm the enemy sent up some coloured rockets from PETIT BOIS but nothing happened. At 7pm the Bn was relieved by the 8th R. DUBLIN FUSILIERS of the 48th Inf Bde. Relief started complete at 9.30 p.m. Bn then proceeded to DONCASTER HUTS (Rd junction L.4. SW of Ln LOCRE Ref. H42c Brick 5A) in Divisional Reserve. Since April 1st our Casualties have been 1 killed 1 died of wounds 17 wounded (many all slight) & all men. From April 15th to 19th the Bn had no casualties whatever, the enemy being unusually quiet. During the whole tour (April 15th to 19th) the enemy next were no French mortars at all, which is unusual for this part of the front.	

A3834 Wt. W4973/M687 750,000 8/16 D. D. & L. Ltd. Forms/C.2118/13.

WAR DIARY
or
INTELLIGENCE SUMMARY

7th LEINSTER   Army Form C.2118.

Place	Date	Hour	Summary of Events and Information	Remarks and references to Appendices
	April 20th to April 26th		Nothing of importance occurred. Working parties found amounting daily to 195 other ranks with a proportion of officers. The usual training was carried out with the remainder. 3 N.C.O's WHTNEHEAD & A Coy was detailed for intelligence officer during the period and given 12 men to train as scouts. The duties of these men comprise in addition to the ordinary scouting knowledge, a thorough knowledge of the enemy system in front of the 47th Bde Sector especially that in the PETIT BOIS and BOIS de WYTCHAETE and EAST of the village of WYTCHAETE. The morale of the Battalion is high. The Battalion has never been in better form and there is very little crime, practically nil(?).	
	April 27th and April 28th		Nothing of importance occurred in these days	
	April 29th		The Bn was to proceed on the 30th inst to Back Billets in the neighbourhood of FLETRE, but this was cancelled at the last moment, it is understood that the Bn is to proceed into the lines in the S.W.A.	

A5834 Wt. W4973/M687 750,000 8/16 D.D. & L. Ltd. Forms/C.2118/13.

Army Form C. 2118.

2/LEINSTER REGIMENT

WAR DIARY
or
INTELLIGENCE SUMMARY
(Erase heading not required.)

Place	Date	Hour	Summary of Events and Information	Remarks and references to Appendices
	April 30th		Nothing of importance occurred on this date. The Bn is under orders to proceed to KEMMEL SHELTERS (N.14 d 2,3) at Sheet FRANCE 28 S.W.	

T.R.A. Stannus Lt Col.
Comdg 2nd Leinster Regt

WAR DIARY:
------o0o------

VOLUME:- 18

FOR MONTH OF MAY, 1917.

UNIT:- 7th Leinster Regiment

WAR DIARY or INTELLIGENCE SUMMARY.

Army Form C. 2118

7th LEINSTER

Place	Date	Hour	Summary of Events and Information	Remarks and references to Appendices
	1/5/17		The Bn moved to KEMMEL SHELTERS. 1 Company remained at DONCASTER HUTS. Strength of the Battalion on this day 30 officers 955 other ranks.	
	2nd & 4th		The Bn remained in its position. Nothing of importance occurred. At 9pm on the 3rd instant the gas alarm was sounded and the Bn stood to. It turned out to be a false alarm and the Bn stood down at 9.30pm.	
	5th	5.30 pm	The Bn relieved the 7th R. Irish Rifles in Bde support. Relief was complete at 5.30 pm. Dispositions of the Battalion were then as follows. Bn H.Q. ROSSIGNOL ESTAMINET (N 22 a 2, 5). A Coy. ROSSIGNOL ESTAMINET (with 1 Platoon at FORT MOUNT ROYAL (about N 23 a 15,50). B Coy. SIEGE FARM (N 16 c 80, 95) C Coy. SIEGE FARM with two platoons at SANDBAG VILLA (N 16 d 55, 95). Between 8.30pm and 9pm the enemy started shelling Bock area, directing attention to KEMMEL and R.E FARM (N 15 c 05, 60) which latter place was next a fire and burned for some hours. No casualties.	Ref Map Nt France 1:25000 ed S.A.
	6th		At about 12.30 am The enemy recommenced shelling but did no damage. The day passed quietly. Bn HQ evening about 9pm the enemy commenced shelling again but did no	

… **WAR DIARY** or **INTELLIGENCE SUMMARY.** 7th LEINSTER Army Form C. 2118

Place	Date	Hour	Summary of Events and Information	Remarks and references to Appendices
	7th		damage. Enemy Howitzer in the 2nd Army Area. At 8.45 pm enemy Howitzer gun with exception of 12 inch Howitzers commenced firing and kept it up till 8.50 pm. The enemy retaliated slightly. At about 9.45 pm the enemy commenced shelling both areas again and dropped a few in ROSSIGNOL WOOD immediately to the E of ROSSIGNOL ESTAMINET, but without doing any damage. At 11 pm we shelled the enemy vigorously & till 11.5 pm when we stopped his shelling & the remainder of the day.	
	8th		At about 3 AM the enemy started shelling again. Our guns immediately replied and his fire ceased. 9.4.15 H.A. SPENCE reported his arrival in this day.	
	9th		At about 8 pm the enemy opened an intense bombardment on the 49th Brigade on our left, & to a less extent on our Front. This bombardment lasted about 60 minutes when ceased.	
	10th		The Bn was relieved by the 7th R. Inniskilling Fusiliers at 3.30 pm and	

Army Form C. 21

7th LEINSTER

WAR DIARY
or
INTELLIGENCE SUMMARY.
(Erase heading not required.)

Place	Date	Hour	Summary of Events and Information	Remarks and references to Appendices
	10th		proceeded to DIZON CAMP 1½ of an inch N of the SCHERPENBERG Wind-mill here it remained for the night. This is a very dirty camp and has evidently been much neglected.	
	11th	9.20am	The Bn. paraded at 9.20am and marched to EECKE, where it was billeted in neighbouring FARMS. This was a very trying march owing to the heat.	11.25 00°F 5 m.
	12th		~~[struck through]~~	
	13th	5pm	At 5pm whilst in this day the 2nd LEINSTER REGT arrived in billets immediately N of our own. Each of our messes entertained the corresponding messes of the line Bn to dinner.	
	14th		The 2nd Bn left. We remained in present Billets. A draft of 5 men arrived.	

WAR DIARY
or
INTELLIGENCE SUMMARY

7th LEINSTER

Army Form C. 211

Place	Date	Hour	Summary of Events and Information	Remarks and references to Appendices
	15th		We received our orders for the commencement of the march to the training area. Nothing of importance occurred.	

WAR DIARY
INTELLIGENCE SUMMARY. 7th LEINSTER REGT

(Erase heading not required.)

Army Form C. 211

Place	Date	Hour	Summary of Events and Information	Remarks and references to Appendices
	16th		The Battalion paraded at 9.20 AM and proceeded to LYNDE where it remained the night.	
	17th		The Bn paraded at 10am and proceeded to WIZERNES where it remained the night.	Ref Wizernes SM (Sq no 13)
	18th		The Bn proceeded to the Training area and was billeted as follows:— H.Q. C & D Companies at JOURNY A Coy HAUTE PANNEE B Coy LES BUISSONS. Nothing of importance occurred	
	19th		The Bn was engaged in training for the assault in ground prepared to resemble the WYTSCHAETE sector. The training consisted of 2 days of Bn training and three days of Bde Training.	
	26th		On the 26th the Bde was inspected by the G.O.C. 2nd ARMY, who expressed his confidence in the men allotted to the Bde, being satisfactory carried out	

7th LEINSTER.

WAR DIARY
or
INTELLIGENCE SUMMARY.

Army Form C. 2118

Place	Date	Hour	Summary of Events and Information	Remarks and references to Appendices
	May 27th		The afternoon was devoted to sports held by the 6th R. Irish Regt. The following events were won by the Bn.:— 100yds (officers) 1st, 3rd and 4th places. Relay Race. Wrestling on Horseback. One team of officers and one of men. The Bn. ran its relay race over its 1/2 race (1 mile). The afternoon was devoted to sports.	
	May 28th			
	May 29th to May 31st		The Bn. marched from its billets to PLANE CAMP near the CROIX de POPERINGHE via WIZERNES and STAPLES and BAILLEUL, marching upwards of 20 miles on the 31st. This was a tiring march owing to heat and traffic on the Roads. Nevertheless very few men fell out.	

T.R.A. Stannus Major
for Lt. Col. Cmdg. 7 "Leinster"

SECRET.

WAR DIARY.

FOR MONTH OF JUNE, 1917.

VOLUME:- 19

UNIT:- 7/8 Bn Leinster Regiment

WAR DIARY or INTELLIGENCE SUMMARY

Place	Date	Hour	Summary of Events and Information	Remarks and references to Appendices
Aldershot	June	1	The Battalion remained at BLACK CAMP. All companies turned out for the night & were ordered away from the camp owing to the accidental firing of a Verey light.	
			This day was spent by the Battalion in cleaning LEWIS GUNS & equipment generally. 2nd Lt. J. Roy Laurie rejoined from Base.	
		2	The Battalion remained in the present billets & received orders to be in readiness to move at 3 hours notice. Nothing of importance beyond the usual chilly parade & cleaning the camp & equipment.	
		3	The Battalion marched out to BRIGADE H.Q. at ISLIP BARRACKS & paraded for ceremonial route march and spent a considerable time at 12.30 pm.	
		4	The Battalion marched to MALPLAQUET BARRACKS & the whole of the afternoon was spent in making ready plans of equipment required for the attack & preparation for movement. Lt. Col. HOBBS, LOCKE, Lt. Lt. W. H. proceeded to prepare the relief of the 16 Bn. Liverpool Regiment. Major W. Redmond & Captain Roberts a day or more before. Today he (Lt. Col. Redmond) took over — spent a week at Aldershot & came home on Wednesday 1st of June. Dogs of him not now.	

WAR DIARY
or
INTELLIGENCE SUMMARY.
(Erase heading not required.)

Army Form C. 2118.

Instructions regarding War Diaries and Intelligence Summaries are contained in F. S. Regs., Part II. and the Staff Manual respectively. Title pages will be prepared in manuscript.

Place	Date	Hour	Summary of Events and Information	Remarks and references to Appendices
Thiepval	June 5		"A" and "C" Coy in Headquarters moved into the house designated. Disposition of Regiment as follows:- Headquarters - LUNETTE Dugouts. A Company - FRONT LINE. LARK LANE & ASHE POINT. B Company - SUPPORT - PARK LINE. C Company -	
	6	10.30 AM	The enemy shelled BIRR BARRACKS very heavily, much of the enemy's bombardment was aimed at reaching "C" Company of the Battalion but few hit the place of safety. We had no casualties. One man wounded. B & C Coy relieved at 8.45 p.m.	
	7		"A" Battalion took up position at 2.30 a.m., dispositions as follows:- Headquarters LUNETTE DUGOUTS. "A" Coy in front line SOUTH of PETIT BOIS, B Coy in OAK TRENCH, C & D Coy in PARK LINE. We moved off as a Coy commander instructed of movement. Line Park line at 2.30 a.m. the enemy opened a very heavy concentrated fire on our front.	

Army Form C. 2118

WAR DIARY
or
INTELLIGENCE SUMMARY.
(Erase heading not required.)

Place	Date	Hour	Summary of Events and Information	Remarks and references to Appendices
Le Jeune	June 7		at times one company made it impossible to advance than a few yards at a time and every carrier, runner, officer, or runner, the chief report by the Commanding Officer that the parties direct as well as the investigators. The Division was placed in support of the Battalion was unable to follow on to the attack. As the war advance, the Jumping-off party moves slowly forward and made the attack itself. The intention of the officer after an advance in some cases of 4 or 500 yards and no reinforcements of supports to meet his attack. We repulsed several attacks and no reserves were anywhere on the F. Thousands of machine guns had been brought up to [illegible] guns, and all the time, companies were now in the time, 1st Btn and 14th GRENADIER GUARDS and 2nd INFANTRY REG'T on reaching the RED OBJECTIVE, the intention being a great many to melt away from our own. By the direction of the Col. Commanding and our reported casualties (A) of our [illegible] held on "NANCY" LINE but on their other side of the "B" O.B.Line "CROQUE IRISH REG'T" left. None of the Allied 1st NINTH BR. the REDOUBT FIVE were all held on.— Eng. 2 and 20 hours. On the there of the 14th we were known from the West. like BLUE October. the Operations (C) on the ground by the Division a few another reinforced by 2 more Companies and Reserve Brigades from "A" Company had afore, and off. Bn. Lieut. 5 wounded sent to	

WAR DIARY
or
INTELLIGENCE SUMMARY

Army Form C. 2118

Place	Date	Hour	Summary of Events and Information	Remarks and references to Appendices
In the field	June 7		The left Company (D) reached its objective to close up zero + 1 hour 40 mins. The 1st ROYAL MUNSTER FUSILIERS advanced alongside and made the "GREEN" objective at zero + 3 hours 40 minutes. In spite of a very strong and heavy barrage, there from about on gaining its objective. Every little difficulty conditions when on they advanced one into the enemy line of the day. The men were thoroughly exhausted from an company had to halt. The general much march movement of my mingling up every effort and circumstances accounts of high up became much their problems very much may dies of our wounded from our own dump today. Easy to quieted on from shelling the tank reinstation an exception CAPTAIN ACTON M.C. wounded, would not relinquish his command until the Headquarters dugout. CAPT. JA. FARELL came in command and appointed LIEUT A.F. WHITEHEAD his adjutant. Details of prisoners etc taken in rear explained about 50 prisoners or so as a result of my section. The enemy amongst French. Party of fifteen enemy captured by sin. On nearing of refugees or targets.	
			Casualties—	
			4 machine guns	
			2 trench mortars	
			4 machine gun mountings	
			1 L.T. dugout	
			1 Dugout	

Army Form C. 2118

WAR DIARY
or
INTELLIGENCE SUMMARY.
(Erase heading not required.)

Instructions regarding War Diaries and Intelligence Summaries are contained in F. S. Regs., Part II. and the Staff Manual respectively. Title pages will be prepared in manuscript.

Place	Date	Hour	Summary of Events and Information	Remarks and references to Appendices
[illegible]	Jan 7		Our casualties during the attack were 8 officers wounded, 18 other ranks killed and 92 other ranks wounded. The officers wounded were:— Major J.R.R. Stamer 2/Lieut A.H. Robb 2/Lieut J.P. Parry 2/Lieut W.F.V. Hamilton Lt Buchanan Capt E.P. Hawkshaw L.A.M.C. (Officer who tended them, wounded whilst doing so) Capt E.L. Acton 2/Lieut C. Magary Lieut W. Morris 2/Lieut D.M. Delany	

Army Form C. 2118

WAR DIARY
or
INTELLIGENCE SUMMARY.
(Erase heading not required.)

Instructions regarding War Diaries and Intelligence Summaries are contained in F. S. Regs., Part II. and the Staff Manual respectively. Title pages will be prepared in manuscript.

Place	Date	Hour	Summary of Events and Information	Remarks and references to Appendices
L Hofre	June 7		The Battalion moved in support Bearer at LUNETTE On 7th The Bn Coy on 12" avery tight bombardment the night at along U. bases wherever replies to effective. CAPT SINGLETON being wounded by a piece.	
		8	The Bn. continued tour of trenches from the line and moved out the forenoon as at TRALEE a siness into the centre at 1 p.m.	
		10	The Battalion remained in front lines and continues the work	
		11	An evacuation of from B.G.s. another were present in O.P. at several - morning & in the 12th. Nothing of importance occurred in the situation	
		12	The Battalion continued to hold out in front lines & were relieved	
		13	On ELVERSTEGNE (relieved arrived about 12.30 pm)	
		14	The Bozolin remained in bells at OULTERSTEENE and continued the voice training. Nothing of importance occurred.	
		15	The Bottalin went to the firing wire a few hrs believed DONCASTER HUTS LOOSE and received lectures the about 7.30 pm. Nothing of importance occurred.	
		16	The Battalion marched to METERN Training Base, proceeded to OULTERSTEENE on march route arrived at OULTERSTEENE at 12.00 pm. On eastward of the railroad in the tonit. Weather very dry. MAJOR FEASTAGNUS drew guards recent mach of the promised.	
	20		The 16 Division XIth Divn Commanded 19, 2nd Bn Hampsworth. Lt H O'Carry	

A 5834 Wt W4975/M687 750,000 8/16 D.D. & L. Ltd. Forms/C.2118/13.

WAR DIARY
or
INTELLIGENCE SUMMARY.
(Erase heading not required.)

Army Form C. 2118.

Place	Date	Hour	Summary of Events and Information	Remarks and references to Appendices
In the field	June 18		The Battalion remained in DULLUKENTEPE and arrived at the N. end of camp at Heidjelik Hosferin 18.00 hrs. Nothing of importance occurred. 2/LIEUT A.H. ROBINSON on 18/4.	
	19		2/Lieut F.B. Hunt left the Battalion for the MERSIS AREA on Hospital Ship proceeding via MALTA to the BASE.	
	20		Training area and cordeslaid. Some attached personnel N.W. of GODELMEROVE DE rejoined.	
			During the bombardment these and 3 Btns N. of Ordosu Dere N. E. of Gruneau were very dangerous. Troops & bombguns.	
	21		The Battalion remained in place above. Nothing of importance occurred.	
	22		The Battalion provided working parties on the BERINGTEPE a Dola ja area 12 miles the walnuts continues in [illegible] branch at the depot without cessation. The bivouac at SHAM are all at the destination at 4 p.m. - 12 noon. Chartered for 317 the Balaz Dagh horses flocks 42 m. the wrecks.	
	23		The Battalion remained in [illegible] it provides hills and second on working	
	24		Todd laying nothing to record assumed then.	
	25		Training. Nothing of importance occurred on this date. 2/LIEUT T.C. Murphy reported duty to this Battalion from a reinforcement ? [illegible]	
	26		The Battalion was inspected by the G.O.C. XIX Corps Lt-Gen [illegible] satisfied at the 17 [illegible] men. [illegible] mentioned the exception of being in valleys hardly a breath of air at this time of the year in constantly Hill Unit. Lot 80% are suffering greatly just the warmth. I'm sure by BRIGADIER GENERAL G. PEREIRA, and orders from 4 INF BRIGADE E. It 2nd Bn 2nd Army's of the handing over by the BATTN to LOOS which will take place tomorrow Gen. W.P. Hickie Commands 16 (IRISH) DIVISION Brig Gen.	

A 5834 Wt.W4973/M687 750,000 8/16 D. D. & L. Ltd. Forms/C2118/13.

WAR DIARY or INTELLIGENCE SUMMARY

Army Form C. 2118.

Place	Date	Hour	Summary of Events and Information	Remarks and references to Appendices
In the field	Jan 26		The undermentioned Officers proceeded to the unit, reported and were posted to Coys:- 2/LIEUT GEOFFREY MARCUS EVANS-JACKARD, 2/LIEUT DAVID MARDEN LEMON and 2/LIEUT CHARLES J. EVANS on ASHE. The undermentioned Other Ranks and men returned from detachments or hospitals & rejoined the Battalion for duty during the above a/m period :- 2/LIEUT J. FARRELL MC, LIEUT JE PARKES, LIEUT N.A. LYONS, 2/LIEUT A.H. WHITEHEAD, 2/LIEUT W.H. COADE, 2/LIEUT W. JOHNSTON, 2/LIEUT E.D. GARLAND, 2/LIEUT C.H. MAHANY and 2/LIEUT V.C.G. WHELAN, No 4390 R.S.M. F. CLARKE, No 7216 Sgt T. CUMMISKEY, No 10790 Sgt T. FISHER, No 4282 Sgt P. MOLLOY, No 10020 Sgt J. McKENNA, No 4939 Cpl E. HANLIN, No 2500 4916 Cpl T. CORMACK, No 52 Pte A. DEEGAN, No 2614 Pte H. KEELEY, No 2223 Pte P. COSGROVE, No 7378 Pte A. TIERNEY, No 1711 Pte P. CONROY, No 2974 Pte P. MURPHY, No 3889 Pte M. BULMAN, No 11114 Sgt J. HAMILL and No 16368 Pte P. HOGAN.	
	27		Battn. remained in the present billets – no 1 parade – preparing for demon- stration on next day.	
	28			
	29		The undermentioned Officers reported for duty from hospital:- Capt. J.R. MOSTYN RGFE and 2/LIEUT M.J. KELLY. The Strength of Bn. OR was 1 CO Ms, 1897 and 14 OR.	

Army Form C. 2118.

WAR DIARY
or
INTELLIGENCE SUMMARY

(Erase heading not required.)

Instructions regarding War Diaries and Intelligence Summaries are contained in F. S. Regs., Part II. and the Staff Manual respectively. Title Pages will be prepared in manuscript.

Place	Date	Hour	Summary of Events and Information	Remarks and references to Appendices
L. Hafield	Jan 30		The Battalion remained in its present billets. The weather was fine. Mayor J.J. McIntyre O.C. "C" Company. Lt. Col. Major T. Mather, Lieut A.H. Rooney & 2/Lieut E.J. Smith, & Lieut W. McCarthy, & Lieut N. Retter & Lieut G.D. Boyne. Major Mather proceeding on embarkation.	

E. A. M. Buckley, Lieut Colonel
Comdg 7th (S) Battn. Leinster Regt.

HEADQUARTERS
16TH (IRISH) DIVISION.

G. O. C.,
   47th Infantry Brigade
....

       TO MORROW IS THE FIRST ANNIVERSARY OF THE FIRST RAID WHICH WAS CARRIED OUT BY THE 16TH DIVISION. I FEEL THAT I MUST SEND MY CONGRATULATIONS TO YOU AND TO YOUR BRIGADE STAFF AND TO THE OFFICERS AND N.C.O's AND MEN OF THE 7TH LEINSTERS, NOT ONLY FOR SETTING SO FINE AN EXAMPLE ON THE NIGHT OF JUNE 26TH 1916, BUT ALSO FOR HAVING THROUGH A WHOLE YEAR OF CONSTANT WARFARE, MAINTAINED (AND INDEED I MAY SAY "INCREASED") THE OFFENSIVE SPIRIT WHICH GAVE THE DIVISION ITS FIRST SUCCESS.

       GUILLEMONT AND WYTSCHAETE WERE NATURAL RESULTS OF LOOS AND ITS CRATERS

       I BEG YOU TO CONVEY TO THE BATTALION THE EXPRESSION OF MY ADMIRATION.

JUNE 25TH 1917.   (SD) W.B. HICKIE, Maj-Gen.,
                       COMMANDING 16TH (IRISH) DIVISION.

7TH. Battn. Leinster Regiment.

ROLL OF OFFICERS PRESENT AT BATTALION DINNER GIVEN AT THE HOSPICE, LOCRE ON JUNE 4TH. 1917.

COPY OF DOCUMENT WHICH WAS SIGNED BY ALL PRESENT.

Rank &	Name	Remarks
Lieut. Colonel	G.A.M. Buckley D.S.O.	
Lieut.	W.A. Lyon	
Captain, Rev.	W.J. McConnell	
2/Lieut.	C.E. Duggan	
Lieut. & Qr.Mr.	J. Davis R.A.M.C.	
Lieut.	G.E. Farrell	
M. Vanderbutt		Belgian Brigade Interpreter.
2/Lieut.	H.A. Spence	
Captain	W. Warburton R.A.M.C.	
2/Lieut.	A.H. Whitehead	
Major	F.H. Jourdain	Connaught Rangers.
Major	T.R.A. Stannus	
	V.J. Chappe	French Interpreter.
Captain	G.D. Watkins R.A.M.C.	
Captain	J.M. Carleton	
Lieut. & Qr.Mr.	C. Beastall	
2/Lieut.	D.M. Delaney	
2/Lieut.	C.H. Magahy	
2/Lieut.	J.K.B. Bayley	
2/Lieut.	A.H. Robb	
Captain	G.H. Gray	
2/Lieut.	J. Ryan	
2/Lieut.	W.H. Wilkie	
2/Lieut.	F.F. Barry	
2/Lieut.	C. Weld	
2/Lieut.	C.L. Fudger	
2/Lieut.	E.D. Garland	
2/Lieut.	W.P. Stidston	
2/Lieut.	W.H. Coade.	

7th. Battn. Leinster Regiment.

ROLL OF OFFICERS PRESENT AT BATTALION DINNER GIVEN AT THE HOSPICE LOCRE, ON JUNE 4TH 1917.

Rank & Name.

Lieut. E.W. Moran.

2/Lieut. D.J. Keating.

Captain J.A. Farrell.

Major W. Redmond Royal Irish Regt.

Capt. Rev.J. Wrafter

        Gabral Ryan D.A.P.C. IX Corps.

Capt. Rev. M. O'Connell Divisional Coy,

Captain V.J. Farrell M.C.

Colonel J. Fisher Late. K.E.O.Goorkha Rifles Sub. Area Commandant.

Lieut. J.O'B. O'Hagan

Spud Always. 7th Leinster Regiment.

J. M.Roche Vagrant. A C.O. to-morrow probably or 2/Lieut.

Mack of the 'orses, 7th Leinsters

Captain E.L.L. Acton

Captain J.E. Swinhoe C.F. 47th Brigade.

2/Lieut. J.C.D. Whelan

2/Lieut. P.I. Kelly.

WAR DIARY.

FOR MONTH OF JULY, 1917.

VOLUME :- 20

UNIT :- 7th Leinster Regiment

7th LEINSTER REGT

WAR DIARY
or
INTELLIGENCE SUMMARY

Army Form C. 2118

Place	Date	Hour	Summary of Events and Information	Remarks and references to Appendices
ERINGHEM	1917 July 1st		A dinner was given by Brigadier General PEREIRA to the men of this Battalion who took part in the raid at St Yvon on 1st July 1916. 7 N.C.Os & men were present.	
	2nd		Normal training carried on.	
	3rd		Battalion sports held at Zeggers Capel. Half time attended some prizes distributed by Major General EMS Strickler CB.	
	4th		The Battalion were inspected at work by the Divisional General who subsequently addressed a Batt'n parade, congratulating them upon their share in the Messines Ridge victory. Trials to find the 16th Division as keen shown with a view to selecting a storm troop, an honour earned by the splendid offensive spirit shown by the Division since it came to France.	
	5.6.7th		Batt'n remained in present space & carried out usual training programme. (8th) Competition for best platoon in marching past & drew about won by No. 13 (2/Lt J.Ryan)	
	7-14		Batt'n remained in present billets & continued training programme.	

WAR DIARY

Army Form C. 2118

Place	Date	Hour	Summary of Events and Information	Remarks and references to Appendices
FRINGHEM	July 15.16		Battn remained in present billets + continued training programme.	
TATINGHEM	17		Battn marched to TATINGHEM Area for special training in attack — via ST OMER a distance of about 15 miles. Weather fine + cool. Very few men fell out. Battn guarded in tents (TATINGHEM CAMP) at	
	18		Battns at special training for attack - morning on rifle range. Divisional General visited Battn at work + presented honours awarded to Officers N.C.O.s + men for battle of WYSCHAETE. The list of awards is as follows, + those present to receive same are marked +	

(Lieut) Major J.R. Stannus   Sgt J. Knight   award
Capt. P.J. Jarrell   2216 A/Cpl McManus   St. S.O. Parchment
Lieut G.E. Farrell   x   2264 — Russell J.   do
2Lt. W.S. Mickson   x   2088 " Scott P.   do
2Lt. R.A. Whitehead   x   1840 " McGuinness H. do
2Lt. E.L. Garland   x   7989 Sgt O'Brien T.   do
2Lt. R.G. Coats   5347 Sgt Marsh J.   do
2Lt. C.H. Magaly   x   5449 A/Cpl Hicks T.   do
2Lt. J.C.D. Whelan   x   5547   Pine   do
                                    5342   Larcombe R.W.
#261 pte Payne. J.   5261 A/Sgt Fenn. J.   M.M.+Parchment
"   Murphy P.   5714 Pte Ferrick P.   Parchment
4885 " Lavery J.   26114   Reilly TC.   do
8711 " Cundy J.   4283 "   Delaney C.   do
7316 Sgt Cunningham T.   5369 "   Billington M. do
4739 R.Q.M Serjeant W   10325 Sgt. Vincent J.H. do
5758 2/Corp Ewan D.   4780 R.S.M. Stanton T. do

Army Form C. 2118

WAR DIARY
or
INTELLIGENCE SUMMARY

(Erase heading not required.)

Instructions regarding War Diaries and Intelligence Summaries are contained in F. S. Regs., Part II. and the Staff Manual respectively. Title pages will be prepared in manuscript.

Place	Date	Hour	Summary of Events and Information	Remarks and references to Appendices
TATINGHEM	July 19 1917		Batln took part in Brigade Scheme of attack over special training area	
	20		" " " " " " " " " "	
			The Div. General watched the operations & at subsequent pow-wow explained the expected rôle of the Brigade in future operations.	
			(Capt. T. J. Harvell)	
			2Lt. C.E. Ash } Proceeded to XIX Corps Reinforcement Depot.	
			2Lt. H.A. Spence }	
			2Lt. M.J. Kelly } Proceeded to 117th T.M. Battery.	
	21		Batln took part in Brigade Scheme of attack.	
	22		Batln resting.	
	23		Batln entrained at STOMER and proceeded to ABEELE STATION from thence	
WINNEZEELE			marched via ABEELE and STEENVORDE to Camp of WINNEZEELE.	
	24		Training under Coy. arrangements. Draft of 8 arrived from Reinforcement Depot.	
WATOU	25		Batln proceeded to WATOU late in evening & were quartered as follows:- A & B Coys in Billets. C & D Coys in tents. Howe Camp.	
	27		Batln took part in Brigade Scheme of attack. The Div. General was present & addressed the officers at the conclusion of operations.	
	28-29		Training under Coy arrangement, weather very unsettled.	

WAR DIARY or INTELLIGENCE SUMMARY

Army Form C. 2118.

(Erase heading not required.)

Place	Date	Hour	Summary of Events and Information	Remarks and references to Appendices
	30 June 1917		The Battalion left Watou and proceeded to No 1 Training area on a Road Party. Bn. arrived at BRANDHOEK CAMP Without incident.	
	31		The Battalion entrained at 4.10 AM at Caestre and proceeded via Poperinghe. Bn. detrained at GOLDFISH CHATEAU about 1 Klo East of YPRES about 5.15 AM. At about 9.15 AM 500 Other ranks and 21 Officers proceeded to POTIJZE CHATEAU in preparation for being a Carrying Party. Owing to the Attack having failed in the morning the Orders were very tardy and confused. There was heavy Enemy Shelling. 2nd LIEUT W.A. WICKES was ordered to Arms and came to the officers mess to follow. 8 Men, 3 wounded and 2 missing. The remainder returned to GOLDFISH CHATEAU at about 6 pm.	

Arthur Tom Colin Col/L
for LIEUT. COLONEL,
COMDG. 7th P.O.W. LEINSTER R.G.

WAR DIARY.

FOR MONTH OF AUGUST, 1917.

VOLUME 21

UNIT 7th Leinster Regiment

Vol 20

Army Form C. 2118.

WAR DIARY
or
INTELLIGENCE SUMMARY

(Erase heading not required.)

1/4 LEINSTER REGT

Place	Date	Hour	Summary of Events and Information	Remarks and references to Appendices
all July	July 1		2/4 Battn. & 4th Gordon. Chateau at 2.30 pm to the dug out prepared in the swampground of the 153rd Bridge. Disposition made as follows:- A Coy as guides to 1, B, C, & top CAMBRIDGE TRENCH. Remainder to other Reserve dugouts.	
	2		The Battalion relieved the 8/10 GORDON HIGHLANDERS, two Companies to the Front line, Buttans Highgate etc. — WILD WOOD "A" Company — "B" Company — "D" Company — "C" Company — IBEX RESERVE & DUGCOTTAGE "Douglas line" which FREZENBERG Reserves.	
			2 LIEUT. A. HROOD got wounded [illegible] Reserves the following 6 Fine at 6:00 am LC.	
	3		The Battn. relieved the 1/4 SEAFORTH HIGHLANDERS in the front line. Disposition on relief the same as the Battn. Headquarters FREZENBERG REDOUBT	

A5834 Wt. W4973/M687 750,000 8/16 D. D. & L. Ltd. Forms/C.2118/13.

WAR DIARY
or
INTELLIGENCE SUMMARY.
(Erase heading not required.)

Army Form C. 2118.

Place	Date	Hour	Summary of Events and Information	Remarks and references to Appendices
In the field	Aug 1	3	"A" Coy — Occupied an Outpost line in front of our FRONT LINE. "B" Coy — ⎫ "C" Coy — ⎬ FRONT LINE "D" Coy — ⎭ — FREZENBERG REDOUBT. Slight ft. Barry and capt movement very mechanical. The Bn. have learnt their work advantageously. Clear & Hot. Casualties для this command one 1 pvte. wd in ankle by shrapnel	
		4	The Bn. reached their billets at 11 o'clock thoroughly dry & during all the operation they performed their duty exceeding well. as a very heavy thunderstorm on the afternoon of July 31st Saturating the men & agreecable [sic] order from Div. HQ brought C.O. to transfer from Brigade Reserve to be camp bivouac of Batn. 1st Div. (Branch 23 or named).	
		5	C.O. Battn. went to give address to ROYAL DUBLIN FUSILIERS On march from BILLIARD TORONTO CAMP, being incomplete about 4 AM.	

A 5834   Wt. W4973/M687   750,000   8/16   D. D. & L. Ltd.   Forms/C.2118/13.

WAR DIARY
or
INTELLIGENCE SUMMARY.

(Erase heading not required.)

Army Form C. 2118

Place	Date	Hour	Summary of Events and Information	Remarks and references to Appendices
In the field	Aug 6	6	Bn. arrived at Toronto Camp, bivouacked in light jack	
		7	shelters. Battalion is now on an hour's notice. Many parties employed	
		8	repairing old camp. Casualties Nil	
		9		
		10		
		11		
		12	Shell of WIEN WOOD tramways buried established	
			"A" Company ATTACHED 107 BDE – Iroken BILLCOTTAGE + shelter IRON RELIEF	
			" B " " –	
			" C " " – WILD WOOD	
			" D " " – For Bn.Gd. YPRES & RAILWAY RGD	
			Carried on the duty of consolidation for period of relief.	
			Battalion remained at Toronto Camp.	
	13		Bn. carried on with preparations and recoveryof 42 & 43 yards.	
			During the day Battalion of enemy & our own planes very busy and during the day in the air.	
			About 6.45 p.m. enemy launched a counter attack on our right, which was very repulsed.	

Army Form C. 2118.

WAR DIARY
or
INTELLIGENCE SUMMARY.
(Erase heading not required.)

Instructions regarding War Diaries and Intelligence Summaries are contained in F. S. Regs., Part II. and the Staff Manual respectively. Title pages will be prepared in manuscript.

Place	Date	Hour	Summary of Events and Information	Remarks and references to Appendices
In the Front	Aug 14		A party of 200 men under 11 officers went out to the RCRE Dump proceeded and beyond the Station at TORONTO CAMP, they came under total 10 mins. Enemy shell fire - of no consequence. 2 other ranks killed & one other Rank three missing	
	15		2th Battalion Hampshire had 2 or 3 other ranks wounded. The horses "C.P." of "D" at 9 noon sent a Lieut & 55 privates of trenches bathe at the tea room RE.	
	16		At 11:10 am the battalion moved up the line back in reserve to the 40 INFANTRY BRIGADE. Disposition on arrival of the various Headquarters. — On the Ghost Street "A" Company — IRSH TRENCH "B" Company — IRSH TRENCH "C" Company — IRSH TRENCH "D" Company — IRSH RESERVE. Casualties 2 other ranks wounded	

A 5834 Wt. W.4973/M687 750,000 8/16 D. D. & L. Ltd. Forms/C.2118/13.

WAR DIARY
INTELLIGENCE SUMMARY.
(Erase heading not required.)

Army Form C. 2118.

Place	Date	Hour	Summary of Events and Information	Remarks and references to Appendices
Northern France	Aug 16		Lt-Adjt I Mallison & 2nd Lt Impey proceeded to the R/S.C.L.M. to Boulogne	
	17		2nd.S.Royal Munster Fusiliers. 2nd Lt. Lt. Cole was wounded.	
			The 9th Brigade Royal Fusiliers is now far in the advance. Battalion in our left front from Fresenberg Road to the Railway, & under Brigade	
	18		2/5 Lancaster Complete about 9 p.m. At 12 noon the Battalion was relieved by the 1/10 Kings Own Scottish Borderers and proceeded to marshalling at Vlamertinghe now over, when the Brig: Maj: the comp'd. commanders & Adjut CEASHE probably received the orders CAPT JM GRAY into bivouac offrs form before midnight. Came too bivouac which is thirs / relieve guards and ... effect relieving	
	19		The Battalion is bivouacked at N11.d... at the line in a received... formation by Brigade & Battn. HQ at N11.C.8.4. arriving there about 10.30 am. D Coy of B Coy furnished a/... then the line.	
	20		The Brigade proceeded to march to ~~ERKE~~ and bivouac at O 23. 6.7.3. "B" Coy furnished ... guards at ... as battn. day	
	21		Brigade remained in its present location, resting, refitting & maintaining outposts	

WAR DIARY or INTELLIGENCE SUMMARY

Army Form C. 2118

Place	Date	Hour	Summary of Events and Information	Remarks and references to Appendices
In the field	Aug.	22	At about 8 a.m. the enemy shelled the vicinity of the Camp with H.2 shells the gun nest appeared to have been firing at a range of about 9 to 11 Kilometres. Casualties 9 damage Nil. The Battalion paraded by march route to CAESTRE at 11.15 a.m. and entrained at 1 p.m. for BAPAUME, arriving at 10.30 p.m.	
		23	At 12.30 a.m. the Battalion proceeded by march route to Camp about 2000 yds North of Achiet-le-Grand (Sheet 57c. A.28 & 7.4) arriving about 2.45 a.m. Ground Rubbs addressed Officers at Anignole H.Q. at 5.30 p.m. The Battalion remained in Camp. The usual programme of training being carried out. Nothing of importance to report.	
		24		
		25	The Battalion left Camp at 11 a.m. & marched to starting point (Sheet 57c. A.18.d.7.5.) having tea at 11.35 p.m. The Battalion marched to Northern Camp, Mayenneville (Sheet 57 B. S.23.c.4.4) arriving about 12.30 p.m. The rest of the day was devoted to the usual matters.	
		26	The Battalion left Camp at 2 p.m. & proceeded by march route to Camp at B.9.a.5.5. (Sheet 57c) arriving at 3.30 p.m.	

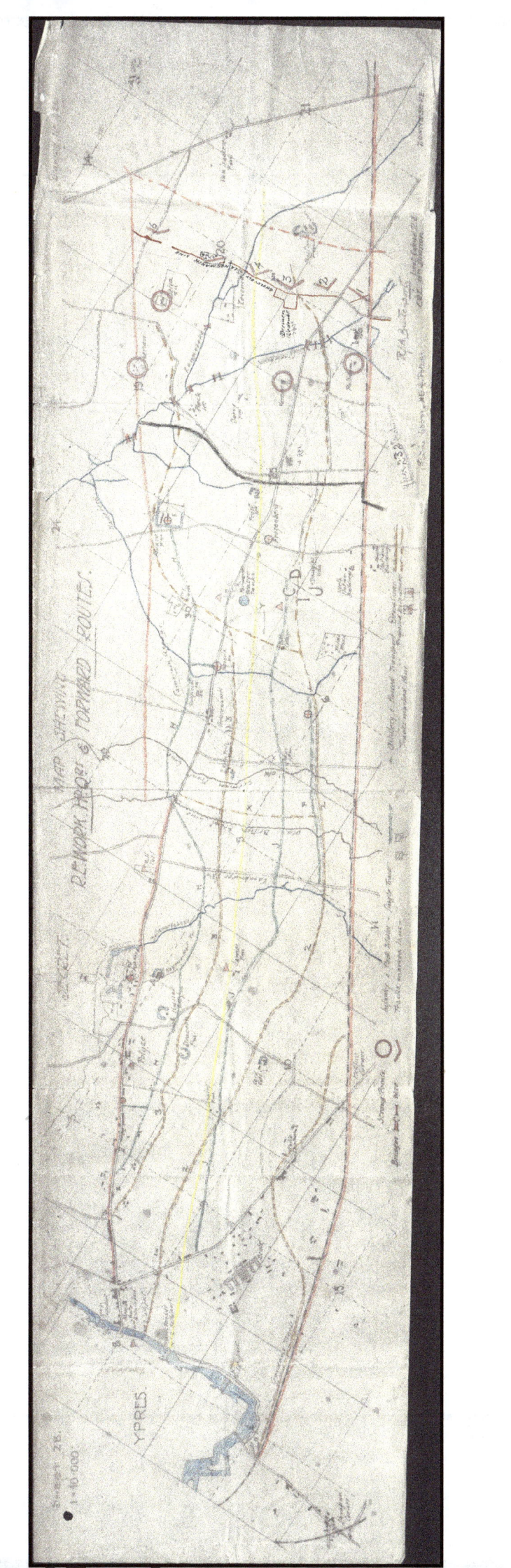

Army Form C. 2118.

WAR DIARY
INTELLIGENCE SUMMARY
(Erase heading not required.)

Place	Date	Hour	Summary of Events and Information	Remarks and references to Appendices
In the Field	Aug	27) 28) 29) 30) 31)	The Battalion remained in camp at B.9.a. 5.5. The usual fatigues. B. coys was carried out daily, & all officers had an opportunity to visit & reconnoitre the new front to be taken over. On 31st a Battalion cross country run was held, "C" by being winners.	

[signature] Lieut.-Colonel
COMDG. 7th P.O.W. LEINSTER R.G.

WAR DIARY.

FOR MONTH OF AUGUST, 1917.

VOLUME 22

UNIT 7th Leinster Regiment,

Army Form C. 2118.

WAR DIARY
or
INTELLIGENCE SUMMARY
(Erase heading not required.)

1/LEINSTER. REGT.

16th DIVISION

Place	Date	Hour	Summary of Events and Information	Remarks and references to Appendices
In the Field	Sept.	1 & 2	The Battalion remained in Pateen Camp B9.a. The usual routine work being carried out daily.	
		3	The Battalion moved off at 7.30 p.m. to relieve the 6th Royal Irish Regt. in the trenches. The march was carried out by Platoons at 5 minute intervals. Disposition:– H.Q. – Railway Reserve U.25.d.50.25. 4 Coys – Front line. "B" Coy – From Junction: Trench & the junction of Valley ? Sap Trenches. "D" Coy – from Valley Trench & Top of Queen's Ave. "C" – from Queen's Ave. & THE LOOP. "A" – THE LOOP.	
		4	There were no casualties. The relief was complete at 11 p.m. The Battalion remained in the front line. Nothing of importance to report.	
		5	Stat in front line. Enemy active on Dury Trench during the afternoon in retaliation for our T.M. bombardment which took place at 2.30 p.m.	
		6	Nothing of importance to report. At 5.45 a.m. an enemy Gun at U.20.b.15.50. opened out a small mortar fire. 1 the enemy (8mm) at U.21.a.4.3 (approx).	

2449 Wt. W14957/M90 750,000 1/16 J.B.C. & A. Forms/C.2118/12.

WAR DIARY
INTELLIGENCE SUMMARY.
(Erase heading not required.)

Army Form C. 2118.

Instructions regarding War Diaries and Intelligence Summaries are contained in F.S. Regs., Part II. and the Staff Manual respectively. Title pages will be prepared in manuscript.

Place	Date	Hour	Summary of Events and Information	Remarks and references to Appendices
In the Field Sept.	7.		Casualties: 1 killed, 1 wounded. The weather which has been fine & warm shews distinct inclination to ...	
	8.		Nothing important occurred. 2/Lt. T.C. Gray reported for duty to Br. N.B.	
	9.		At 8 a.m. 1,000 mortars, dying in every dir. Its line of bombardment. Reasons bombarded the transept trenches with Gas Projectiles for about 15 minutes. As far as could be gathered he suffered a great many casualties & was very quiet during the day. A & B 6 yds which were in the line at that time suffered some casualties - 3 killed 14 men & offrs slightly gassed. Unfortunately 9th Infantry who are 1 to 3 who shell attack it fine he was thought to be slightly gassed. At 9.30 pm an enemy commenced bombarding RAILWAY RESERVE with 77mm 9 no shells. This entailed automatically sht about 10 a.m. when a warning 1 gun was given from front line - ... 1 the field wire still intact. Between 10 & 11 pm enemy sent out large clouds of smoke mingled with gas shells. The smoke was caused by throwing smoke bombs out No Man's Land while the line was subjected to a heavy T.M. and stry bombdt. As numbers jumped of what appeared to be rifle grenades	

Army Form C. 2118

WAR DIARY
INTELLIGENCE SUMMARY
(Erase heading not required.)

Place	Date	Hour	Summary of Events and Information	Remarks and references to Appendices
In the Field	1/1/18	9	Wire sent over as from line. Up above followed. Skirters reported normal at 11.15 p.m. There were no casualties.	
		10	A Quiet day. 2/Lieut HAROLD EDWARD JOSLIN, 15743, Pte EASTON and 55117 Pte GARDNER were killed at 3 p.m. in BOYELLES Cemetery from T.M. R. fire. Ambulance in later. Casualties were reported. She was R knee shell T.M. activity, and some increase in shelling in our own trenches. CAPT. G. H. WATKINS R.A.M.C. (att: 7th Leinster Regt) was awarded the D.S.O. for conspicuous gallant life, and devotion to duty during the period of FREZEN. BERG RIDGE.	
		11	Following a bright day with only one casualty (P. G. MEAGHAN, A Coy, Shot Bomb, G Head of 6 morning (R Hd L.)). Bn. relieved as 1R from his by R. 1st Bn. MUNSTER FUSILIERS (B Rly.) Commencing at 7.30 a.m. Bn. Ba. Prussia the Relief. Coys as keep as follows:	

Bn. HQ U 26 b 8.8 (RAILWAY RESERVE)
A   T 21 d 3.3
B   J 25 b 8.0
C   T 24 b 9.3
H   C 2 a 9.9

(the relief was carried out with one casualty (slightly wounded))

Army Form C. 2118

WAR DIARY
or
INTELLIGENCE SUMMARY.
(Erase heading not required.)

Instructions regarding War Diaries and Intelligence Summaries are contained in F. S. Regs., Part II. and the Staff Manual respectively. Title pages will be prepared in manuscript.

Place	Date	Hour	Summary of Events and Information	Remarks and references to Appendices
RAILWAY RESERVE	12.9.17		An entirely uneventful day. The Battalion remaining in support, occupied its forward working parties to B Front the old entrenching equipment against Headquarters.	
"	13.9.17		Nothing to report. Patrol covered our escort of prisoners reported his return from base, but received instructions from the Bde 47th Inf Bde.	
"	14.9.17		Battalion in support. Nothing to report. Casualties nil.	
"	15.9.17	9 p.m	The Battalion was relieved in support by 60. Conn. RANGERS and proceeded to PATRICIA CAMP (S.9.A.) where it took over the huts etc. recently by the 2nd S.E. Lancs IRISH REGT. The relief was carried out after dark, and no casualties were reported.	
PATRICIA CAMP	16.9.17		Battalion in reserve. DIVINE SERVICE in CHAPPELLERS. Nothing to report. Casualties nil.	
"	17.9.17		Battalion in reserve. Usual routine. Parade at 13.2.5.4.3., 2 to 3 hours. Programmes of training carried out.	
"	18.9.17		Battalion in reserve. Training as above. Major A.H. SEAGRIM D.S.O. and Lieut A.J.FARRELL on Battalion in reserve. Training 3 hours & reports. Nothing to report.	
"	19.9.17		Battalion in reserve. The O.i/c C & (A/D) Coy O.i/c (A/D) to O.Coy as shown in B.16. Order 12(1)	
"	20.9.17 21.9.17			B.O. J-21-9-17 appended
"	22.9.17		Battalion in reserve. Nothing to report.	
"	23.9.17 24.9.17			
"	25.9.17		B.O.C. Division congratulated the recipients of honours for operations E of YPRES at a parade of the Batt. Nothing to report.	
"	25.9.17 (late)		Staff of 36 O.R. arrived.	
"	26.9.17		Battalion in reserve. Training as usual. Nothing to report.	

Army Form C. 2118

WAR DIARY
or
INTELLIGENCE SUMMARY.
(Erase heading not required.)

Instructions regarding War Diaries and Intelligence Summaries are contained in F. S. Regs., Part II. and the Staff Manual respectively. Title pages will be prepared in manuscript.

Place	Date	Hour	Summary of Events and Information	Remarks and references to Appendices
ST. P PATRICIA CAMP.	27.9.17		Battalion resumed draft of 120R arrival. Training as usual.	
	28.9.17		Battalion inspections. Afternoon Batt. Cross Country Race won by B Coy 200 starters.	
	29.9.17		Battn in march order, inspections held prior to going into line, Divines held at Coys stn.	
	30.9.17		" " Nothing to report.	

J M Chalmers Capt
adjt 2 hn

COMMANDING 2nd (S) BN. LEINSTER REGIMENT (R.O.)
LIEUT COLONEL

Part 1.   BATTALION ORDERS   No. 143.
by
Major A.H. Seagrim, Commanding 7th Battalion Leinster Regiment.
In the Field.   21st September, 1917.

1. **ROUTINE.**   Sick parade tomorrow will be at 8 a.m.
                 Orderly Room will be at 2 p.m.

2. **SCHEME.**   A practice attack will be carried out by "A" and "B" Companies at 11-30 a.m. tomorrow for the Divisional Commander's Inspection. "D" Company will arrange for a subsequent counter-attack. The Officers Commanding these Companies will meet the Commanding Officer at 7-45 a.m. to reconnoitre the ground.

3. **HONOURS.**   The Commander-in-Chief has been pleased to award decorations as under to the undermentioned N.C.O's and Men of the Battalion. :-

No.	Rank	Name	Award	Coy.
3421	Pte.	H. Mc'Guigan.	Bar to Military Medal. (M.M.)	"A"
8327	L/C.	W. Atkin	Military Medal.	"C"
10790	Sgt.	T. Fisher.	do	"A"
4282	"	P. Molloy	do	"D"
5191	Cpl.	S. Cox.	do	"A"
2975	Pte.	M. O'Grady.	do	"B"
3459	Sgt.	P. Doyle.	do	"D"
5464	Pte.	J. Gulvin.	do	"B"
1504	"	P. Bootrey.	do	"B"
5828	"	P. McNamara	do	"D"
10436	"	G. Blakeley	do	"C"
5226	"	W. Hewitt	do	"C"
5759	L/C.	A. Gurdier	do	"C"
2829	Pte.	C. Mulhall	do	"A"

4. **FIELD CASHIER.**   For the future the Field Cashier's hours of attendance will be as under:-

PLACE	DAY	TIME.
BRETENCOURT.	DAILY	9.30 a.m. to 12.30 p.m.
		2.30 p.m. to 4.30 p.m.
NEUVILLE-VITASSE.	TUESDAY	10.30 a.m. to 12 noon.
MONUMENT.	WEDNESDAY	10 a.m. to 12 noon.
BEHAGNIES.	WEDNESDAY	2.30 p.m. to 4.30 p.m.
BOYELLES.	THURSDAY	10 a.m. to 12 noon.
BOISLEAUX-AU-MONT.	THURSDAY	10.30 a.m. to 11.30 a.m.
BRETENCOURT.	SUNDAY.	9.30 a.m. to 12.30 p.m.

(VI Corps A/ 1613)

5. **GAS.**   All box respirators will be tested at the Divisional Gas School, ERVILLERS, on the afternoon of Monday, 24th inst, and a gas demonstration arranged in the Camp the following day.
     For this purpose the Transport Officer will detail 1 G.S. Waggon to report at Gas School at 11 a.m. the 25th inst

6. **DIVINE SERVICE**   Mass will be celebrated at 7.15. a.m. to-morrow in the Sergeants' Mess hut and not in ERVILLERS as previously arranged.

7. **Musketry.**   The range at B.2.d.4.3. has now been put into a serviceable condition and may be taken into use by Companies desirous of doing so. The usual precautions must be observed when any firing is in progress.

8. **NAILS IN LININGS OF HUTS.**   The NISSEN BOW huts are lined with thin match boarding which will not hold nails. Nails or hooks to hold equipment etc. are on no account to be driven into the matchboard lining of these huts.

(Authority D.R.O. No 1519 dated 29.9.16))

(sd) J.H.M. Staniforth Captain,
A/ Adjt 7th Bn. Leinster Regt.

WAR DIARY

FOR MONTH OF OCTOBER, 1917.

UNIT 7th Leinster Regiment

VOLUME NUMBER 23

WAR DIARY or INTELLIGENCE SUMMARY

Army Form C. 2118

4th Lincoln Regt

Place	Date	Hour	Summary of Events and Information	Remarks and references to Appendices
[illegible]	1-10-17		The Battn relieved the 6th Bn [illegible] Regt in the front line trenches on nights of 1st & 2nd Oct. The dispositions being A Coy in PARAPET LANE (N22 a 53) being reserve to the 18 & C & D Coys in front. Disposition of each Company as follows:- Disposition now the relief was complete: LEFT SECTOR (Left of Battn Boundary to Point [illegible]) A Coy + 1 Sec 1st Line B Coy CENTRE [illegible] RIGHT [Reserve Reserve to Point 18 in VALLEY] C & 1 Sec D Coy Bn HQ was [illegible] to Right 12 Company HQ — Bn Headquarters in RAILWAY RESERVE U20 c 50.25	
	2-10-17		[illegible] a quiet day — some shell in B Coy unknown until late [illegible] A2 & PARAPET [illegible] along VALLEY TRENCH & [illegible] was opened 1 man slightly wounded	
	3-10-17		A quiet day — a little enemy artillery. The [illegible] numbered TUNNELL TRENCH and PRACTICE MEETS with the object of drawing enemy's barrage. This object was not achieved and no enemy barrage came down. STRAY SHORTS in QUEENS LANE but no material damage was done. Over the hill	
	4-10-17		During night shots were occasionally fired. RED lights from the trenches no other followed. Enemy patrol seen on MARTIN R. A quiet day.	

WAR DIARY
or
INTELLIGENCE SUMMARY.

(Erase heading not required.)

Army Form C. 2118.

Instructions regarding War Diaries and Intelligence Summaries are contained in F. S. Regs., Part II. and the Staff Manual respectively. Title pages will be prepared in manuscript.

Place	Date	Hour	Summary of Events and Information	Remarks and references to Appendices
In the Line	5.10.17		Morning quiet. During afternoon the enemy was shelling in neighbourhood of enemy front system. TM's: Stokes + Machine Gun Barrage S.O.S. retaliation sent up. 8.07 p.m. Left Brigade fired S.O.S. rockets, which was taken up by Artillery, fire, & barrage fell on 6009 VALLEY TRENCH and Junction of PELICAN AVENUE and BULL Rd. No material damage done. Casualties nil.	
	6.10.17		A quiet day. During afternoon TM's Stokes fired bursts of ammunition — line + hostile MERU with good effect. 9.30 p.m. enemy put 5.9 shell near railway. Enemy TM action against D.26.c.9.2 at 5.5 am - no damage - and later 10 am & 11 am against Junction of STAFFORD LANE and BAUMANS SUPPORT. When he obtained 1 direct hit on Trench Works. Position very satisfactory towards enemy. 2nd Lt J.E. DUFFIELD reported.	
	7.10.17		Quiet day. Very quiet. Own TM's 'STOKES' bombarded enemy line + MEBYS from 12:35 p.m. till 1.25 p.m. Shelled recent enemy relief against LOOP and Trench. Heavy TM's damage 5 Ag.2.S. at 9.15 p.m. Many killed) RAILWAY RESERVE unit 15 men hit & getting into roadway.	
	8.10.17		Morning quiet. The Battalion was relieved in the line in the evening by the 1st ROYAL MUNSTER FUSILIERS, and went into Support in Railway Reserve.	

P.T.O

Army Form C. 2118.

WAR DIARY
INTELLIGENCE SUMMARY.
(Erase heading not required.)

Place	Date	Hour	Summary of Events and Information	Remarks and references to Appendices
In the Support	9/10/17		dispositions — H.Q. O. Cy. 2 Platoons D. Coy } RAILWAY RESERVE (SOUTH) 2 Platoons D. A B } RAILWAY RESERVE (NORTH) The relief was completed by 11 p.m. without casualties.	
	10/10/17		The Battalion remained in support & furnished the usual working parties for the front line. Nothing of importance to report.	
	11/10/17		Battalion in Support. Nothing to report. 4/Lt. H.A. HOWES joined unit.	
	12/10/17 13 14		} Battalion in Support. Nothing of importance occurred during these days preparations were made for their in enemy's line.	P.T.O

Army Form C. 2118.

WAR DIARY
or
INTELLIGENCE SUMMARY.
(Erase heading not required.)

Place	Date	Hour	Summary of Events and Information	Remarks and references to Appendices
In Support	15/10/17 16/10/17		At 2.10 a.m. after a few minutes Artillery bombardment we carried out a raid on the enemy's front line between D'14 d.25.00 and V20 d. 80.40. The party comprised Capt. R.A. DENCH, M.C., Lieuts. DUFFIELD and MAGAHY and 2/Lt. RYAN. 2 prisoners were taken & considerable casualties inflicted on the enemy in his dug-outs. We had 1 man killed and Lt. MAGAHY & 2/Lt. RYAN and several men wounded. 2/Lt. RYAN returned to duty the following day. The party was accompanied by Major Hilbas of 158th by. R.E. who obtained valuable information which enemy trench 9 marks in addition to that supplied by the prisoners. They belonged to 1st. Bav., 228th. R.I.R., 49th. Res. Div.	
	17/10/17		Enemy artillery active during morning on batteries in MAIDA VALE. The Battalion was relieved in support by the 6th. Connaught Rangers and proceeded to PATRICIA CAMP. C.S.M. HICKIE re-commenced and posted to A. Coy.	
	18/10/17 – 24/10/17		Battalion remained in PATRICIA CAMP (B.21.a.8.2.) but supplied parties to work on DURROW CAMP in connection with the 6th. Inniskillings. Training was also carried out by the coys. to completion.	

Army Form C. 2118

Instructions regarding War Diaries and Intelligence
Summaries are contained in F. S. Regs., Part II.
and the Staff Manual respectively. Title pages
will be prepared in manuscript.

WAR DIARY
INTELLIGENCE SUMMARY.
(Erase heading not required.)

Place	Date	Hour	Summary of Events and Information	Remarks and references to Appendices
DURROW CAMP	25/10/17		The day was occupied in moving to DURROW CAMP. The move being completed by 4.30 p.m.	
"	26/10/17		Battalion occupied on Fatigue about the Camp. S/Lt. J.M. CARLETON proceeded to ENGLAND to take up a position as Instructor to the U.S. Army, and LIEUT. WHELAN left on transfer to R.F.C. 2/Lt DUGGAN proceeded to GRANTHAM on a course prior to transfer to M.G.C.	
"	27/10/17		Battalion occupied on fatigues about the Camp.	
"	28/10/17		Divine Service Parades in the morning. Fatigues in the afternoon.	
"	29/10/17		Usual fatigues carried out. Route to Brigade Assembly Pnt. reconnoitred during the day.	
"	30/10/17 31/10/17		Battalion employed in training according to programme, and fatigues about the Camp.	

P.W. Lennon 2/Lt
for Adjutant 7th Leinster Regt.

~~Major General, G.S.~~

G.S.O. (I). (a).

G.S.O. (I). (b).

G.S.O. (II).

G.S.O. (I)., Int.

G.S.O. (III).

G.S.O. (III).

G.S.O. (III).

Chem. Adviser.

Major Kingsford

Capt. Fagan.

Date 25.10.17

SECRET

FILE No. **G.12**

Sub-Nos. 146,

SUBJECT. MINOR OPERATIONS.

Sub-head. Raid by 7th Leinster Regt.

16th October, 1917

VI Corps

16.

Referred to	Date.	Referred to	Date.

SECRET.   Third Army No.G.12/146.

VI Corps.

16th Div. No. A.S. 1239/84   19/10/17.

        I forward the Battalion report on a small raid carried out in the early morning of the 16th instant by a party of 100 men of the 7th Leinster Regt. and I have attached a copy of the Brigadier-General's (47th Inf.Bde.) covering letter.

        The raid in itself calls for no remarks. The scheme was an unpretentious one and had for its main objects the reconnaissance of TUNNEL TRENCH and NO MAN'S LAND and the securing of an identification.

        The R.E. reconnaissance of TUNNEL TRENCH has produced valuable results. A copy of report by the senior R.E. Officer who accompanied the party is attached marked 'B'. This in conjunction with air photographs and the evidence of prisoners will give good ground work for future plans.

                                    (sd) W.B.HICKIE.

                                          Major-General,
                                    Commanding 16th Division.

2.

Third Army.

        A well carried out small raid reflecting credit on all concerned. The information brought back by Major HOLBROW, R.E., is of value.

                                    (sd) A.HALDANE, Lt-Gen.
22/10/17.   Commanding VI Corps.

3.

VI Corps.

        A very good and very valuable raid.

        The information has been most useful.

24/10/17   (sd) J.BYNG, General.

H.Q. VI CORPS.
G.X. 313/97.

16th. Division.

The following remarks by the G.O.C? VI CORPS. and G.O.C., Third Army regarding the report forwarded under 16th. Division A.S. 1239/84 dated 19th. October, are forwarded for information.

By G.O.C? VI CORPS.

"A well carried out ~~xxkxxxxx~~ small raid reflecting credit on all concerned. The information brought back by Major HOLBROW R.E. is of value."

By G.O.C. Third Army.

"A very good and very valuable raid. The information has been most useful".

VI CORPS.
26/10/17

(Sd) E.R. CLAYTON. Major.
For B.G.G.S.

47th. Infantry Brigade.

I have already sent my appreciation to O.C. 7th. Leinsters. I do so again on having obtained the praise of the Corps and Army Commander.

(Sd) W.B. HICKIE, Major-General
27th. Oct. 1917. Commanding 16th. Div.

TO O.C.
7th. Leinsters

I have much pleasure in sending you enclosed for retention.

(Sd) G. Pereira, Brig. Genl.
28/10/17 Commanding 47th. Inf. Bde.

SECRET.   47th Inf. Bde. No. G. 4463.

16th Division.

I attach report on successful raid by 7th Leinsters on night 15/16th October.

The objects were:-

(i) To identify Unit opposite us.
(ii) To get exact description of TUNNEL TRENCH with its entrances.
(iii) To harass enemy, keep up offensive spirit of our troops.
(iv) To avoid casualties and not give away identifications.

All these objects were secured.

The suggestion of using cylinders of compressed air to feign gas emanated from Major LE BUTT, D.M.G.O. 16th Division. Thise ruse proved eminently successful and we caught the enemy with his gas masks on. For the future he will be in doubt when to wear them, or he will believe that we have been inoculated with gas and no longer require masks.

The greatest credit is due to the 177th Artillery Brigade for the barrage they put up. All who went over were loud in their praise for its accuracy and effectiveness.

The 47th M.Gun Company, assisted by the 48th and 49th M.Gun Companies and the 76th M.Gun Company on the right put up a most effective barrage, whilst the 47th T.M.Battery cooperated with Stokes on the flanks.

The medical arrangements, arranged by Colonel CUMMINS, A.D.M.S. 16th Division and Lieut-Colonel BELL, 111th F.A., were the best I have ever seen.

Major HOLBROW and his party of sappers from the 156th Field Coy., R.E. did invaluable work in examining TUNNEL TRENCH, and obtaining complete measurements.

The greatest credit is due to Lieut. Colonel BUCKLEY, Commdg. 7th Leinsters, Major SEAGRIM, O.C. Enterprise, and Capt. DENCH, who trained and led the raiding party for the way in which they planned out the scheme. They were ably assisted by Capt. LAMBERT, who was Acting Brigade Major, 47th Infantry Brigade. No details were forgotten and everything worked like clockwork.

/ I wish

I wish especially to draw attention to the way in which the party were formed up before the raid in the Sunken Road in NO MAN'S LAND in just sufficient time without having a long wait. Also to the fact that everything was brought back, excepting one revolver which got caught in the wire, and could not be extracted. The saving of loss in revolvers by wearing them on a lanyard is very important.

The 49th Reserve Division appears to be of very poor morale. They mostly bolted into the TUNNEL, and as the party had orders not to go into it, this accounts for the few number of prisoners.

The result of the enterprise has increased, if possible, the confidence of the men in their own efficiency, and tends to keep up the fighting spirit of this Battalion. It is the proud boast of the Leinsters that they have always succeeded in their attacks and that no Hun has ever entered their trenches except as a prisoner.

18-10-17.
(sd) G. PEREIRA, Brigadier General, Commanding 47th Infantry Brigade.

HINDENBURG LINE

Sketch shewing typical entrance to tunnel with fire recesses in TUNNEL TRENCH 51B U.20.b.

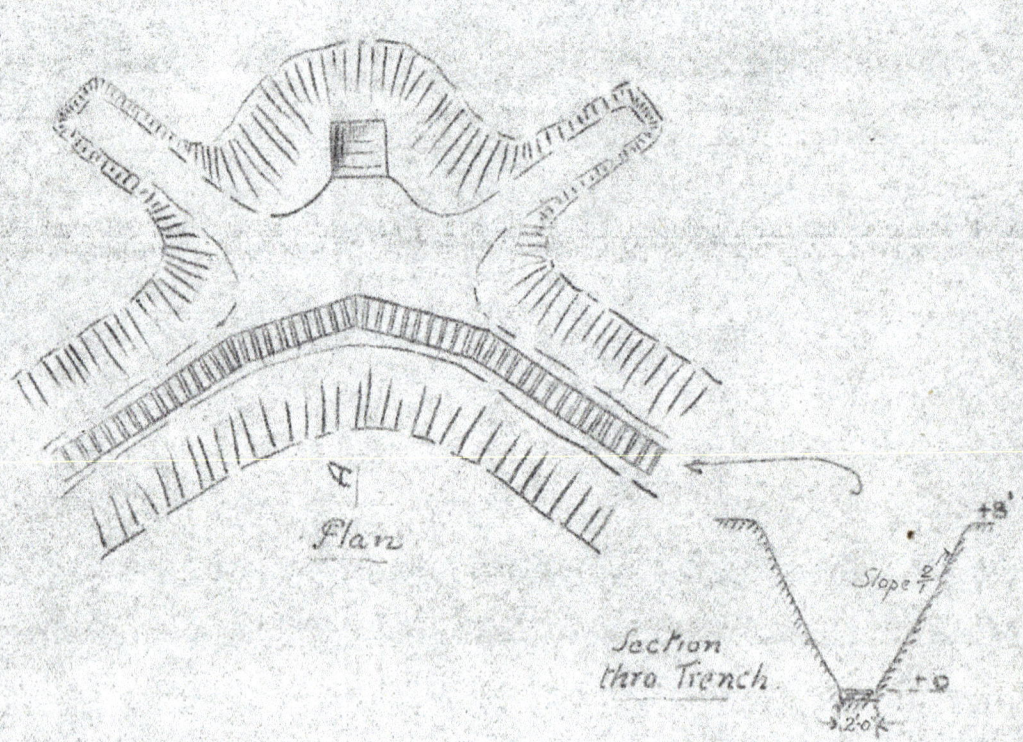

Plan

Section thro. Trench

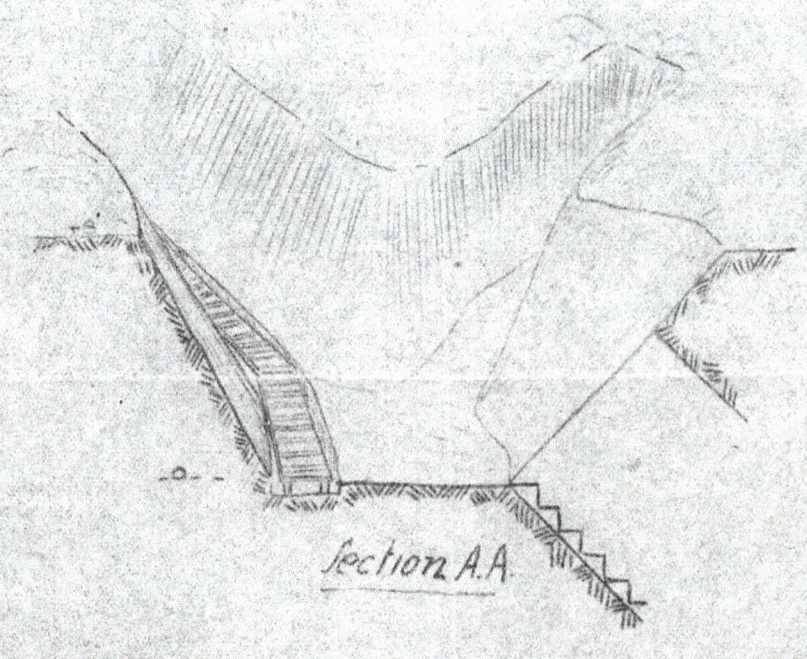

Section A.A.

To accompany report of Major T.L.S. Holbrow. R.E.   16.10.17

SECRET (B)

Report on TUNNEL TRENCH-51.b.U.20.b.

Three parties of R.E. went with the Infantry parties which actually entered the trench.

I myself went with the Southern Party and was in for about 20 minutes. Sgt. NORMANTON took the Northern Party, which was only in the Trench for a few minutes, and corroborates some of the information gained in the Southern Sector. The third party never reached their objective (the MEBUS SAP).

The information is therefore gathered almost entirely from the section of trench from U.20.b.40.75 to U.20.b.33.90.

There were three entrances to the tunnel in this section.

Trench between Tunnel entrances.

Between the entrances to the TUNNEL the trench was purely a "TRAVEL" trench. There were fire points at each tunnel entrance.

The "TRAVEL" trench was 7'6" to 8' 0" deep.
The bottom was about 2' wide and duckboarded for most of its length. The duckboards appeared fairly old. The sides of the trench were nowhere revetted and sloped at about a 2/1 slope. Between the fire posts no firing steps were put in, and with the exception of a few places where old saps, closed up, made gaps in the side of the trench, the parapet could not be used as a fire parapet.
The intervals between the fire posts were traced back to form traverses, but they were of such insufficient depth front to rear and the trench was so broad that by leaning against the parados one could see an adjacent tunnel entrance from a point opposite any one of the three tunnels examined.

The trench bore very few signs of recent shell fire and, owing to its large cross section, sloping sides and the absence of revetment, I think even prolonged shelling would not block it. The trench might become merely a scoop in the ground but would, I think, be passable and sufficiently deep to afford covered passage.

The walls will, I think, subside in the winter, but I do not think this opinion should be taken as tending to show that the Bosch intends evacuating the line.

The bottom was quite dry and a considerable amount of subsidence might take place in the sides without rendering the trench unfit for use. This type of trench is uncomfortable and muddy in winter but requires comparitively little upkeep.

The trench provided poor cover even from shrapnel and enfilade machine gun fire.

Fire Posts.

The tunnel entrances were from 2 to 4 feet forward from the duckboards, the side of the trench being dug out into a sort of semi-circular bowl from each side of which was dug a recess about 4' x 4' x 4'6" deep projecting out at an angle to the trench. These recesses had no parados and one shell landing in front of the tunnel entrance would stand a good chance of

/ killing

killing the occupants of both recesses and destroying the entrance at the same time.

Each recess had a box of "truncheon" bombs let into the side at about two feet below ground level and an enormously heavy steel ~~breastkiek~~ breastplate stood on the parapet of each. Two of these which I looked at were rusty and had apparently been standing some time as they had sunk some inches into the mud.

There was no revetment or trenchboarding in these recesses or in the open space before the dugout.

Shafts to Tunnel.

The shafts to the tunnel were of normal size and timbering.

Close timbered with the cases set at right angles to the slope and steps nailed on. Nothing was done to finish off the entrance nor was the surrounding bank revetted with the result that in one case mud was flowing down the shaft. This would occur a lot in winter.

Some of the infantry spoke of half doors and gas curtains in the shafts.
One entrance was certainly covered with a kind of sacking but my impression is that these coverings were rather weather proof than gas proof.

The shafts appeared at least 20' deep, possibly more. Smoke from bombs and "P" bombs made it difficult to judge. Slope about 1/1.

The topsill of one dugout was crashed in at the top by shell fire. The timbers looked new.

The distance between the entrances was measured with a tape and found to be 28 yards and about 20 yards.

The positions of these fireposts is easily distinguished on the photos and in most cases the recesses can also be seen. Some of the dugout entrances slope back at about 45°, they would be visible in a highly magnified aeroplane photograph taken ~~from xxxxxxxxxxxxxxxxxxxxxx~~ vertically above or better still at an angle from the back of the trench.
The heads of the shafts had from 4' to 5' of earth on top of them; in no case could I see any burster or concrete cap.

I think each shaft had a sentry on top, possibly on account of the gas alarm and the fact that these men made for the entrances and downstairs seems to point to an underground communication either with the rear or flanks, or both, as men caught in a trench in raids usually clear out over the back of the trench rather than down a dugout which is certain to be bombed.

From CRUMP ALLEY being allowed to fall in rather points to the same thing.

I could find no trace of shafts behind the trench nor were there any tracks or trenches leading in from the rear. In fact it was difficult matter to get up the parados side of the trench.

/ There was

There was a good number of small shallow saps and cross trenches in front of the main trench but they did not seem to have been used at all.

I saw no wires going down into the dugout entrances, but omitted to note this point particularly. We cut two wires on entering the trench which appeared quite new and were simply thrown down on the parapet. It would appear that the Bosch had telephonic communication with the rear (possibly from MARS) as during the last 10 minutes in the trench a good many bursts occurred near the trench. Most of these were bombs from the sap to MARS but some were undoubtedly shells, suggesting that his guns knew where we were.

The timbering of one of the shafts was burning in one place, about half way down when we left.

One man was crouching on the parapet just by the junction of the main trench and the sap to MARS. A dugout is marked here, possibly he was the sentry over this.

I should say about 8 or 12 men were firing from the MEBUS Sap. Whether they came from the MEBUS or whether there is an entrance to the tunnel here, I could not say.

German M.G's.

I noticed no German machine guns firing at all.

Wire.

The wire was cut to ribbons. I came upon one thick barbed wire concertina about 2' high. It formed no obstacle as it was not fastened to pickets. A few of the shell holes had loose wire thrown in but this formed a very poor obstacle.

Old C.T's in NO MAN'S LAND.

Going over and coming back I looked for traces of the communication trenches which appear across NO MAN'S LAND on the air photo. I saw no recognizable trace of these. One N.C.O. thought he saw a bit of one, but this is doubtful. The ground is so full of shell holes that, should it be necessary to dig across NO MAN'S LAND, partial cover can very quickly be got by linking up the craters.

Field of Fire.

There seemed to have been no effort to flatten the parapets and the foreground was very much obscured by heaps of earth thrown up by shells. I think a man would have a expose himself a great deal to get a good field of fire.

The man using the recesses would be firing across rather than straight to the front.

In bombing down the trench care would have to be taken that splinters of Mills bombs did not fly back and hit the bayonet men owing to the inadequacy of the traverses. The recesses form good bomb posts for trench blocks.

/ Bombers on

Bombers on the parapet would show up against the sky very plainly owing to the depth and sloping sides of the trench.

As before mentioned there are German bombs in all recesses, on the right hand side, quite easily found.

The Germans appeared to have little fight in them, confining themselves to throwing bombs from their trench and using their rifles.

16/10/17. (sd) T.L.S. HOLBROW,
Major R.E.

ENTERPRISE BY
7th BATTALION LEINSTER REGT.

ZERO. 2.10 a.m. 16th October, 1917.

OBJECT. Identification and reconnaissance of TUNNEL TRENCH from U.14.d.25.05 to U.20.b.36.80.

COMPOSITION. 5 Officers and 100 Other Ranks with 1 Officer and 12 Other ranks R.E. divided into 5 parties viz:- "A", "B", "C", "D" and "E".

PREPARATION. Wire cutting by artillery and T.Ms for 4 days previous to Zero according to programme. Patrols previously reconnoitred gaps in wire and laid a guide line of black telephone wire.

POINTS OF DEPARTURE. U.20.b.15.60 and U.20.b.00.85 (MARTIN ROAD).

REPORT. At Zero - 15 minutes all parties with the exception of "E" were in their allotted positions in MARTIN ROAD. Party "E" was kept in reserve in our front line trench.

At Zero minus 1 minute on a signal being fired (three Red Very Lights) from advanced Battalion H.Q. in QUEEN'S LANE 30 cylinders of compressed air were opened and "P" bombs lighted to simulate a gas attack.

At Zero the Artillery, M.Gun and T.M. barrage opened on the enemy's front line and strong points, the shooting being very accurate and most effective. The enemy fired one green Very Light from the direction of MARS (U.20.b.22.88), and gas signals could be heard from the enemy's lines.

Simultaneously the parties moved forward meeting with no obstacles and were able to get close to our barrage.

At Zero plus 2 minutes the barrage lifted from the portion of trench selected for attack to a line 200 yards in rear of it thus forming a box barrage.

Party "A" immediately entered the enemy trench at U.20.b.37.83, formed a block just South of this point, remainder of party proceeding up the trench towards the MARS sap (U.20.b.22.88).

Officers leading parties "B", "C" and "D" had by this become casualties and the N.C.O. in charge of "C" finding the garrison of MEBU MARS (U.20.b.22.88) offering strong opposition led his party into the German trench and reported to O.C. "A" party.

Party "B" met with heavy fire and bombing from MARS (U.20.b.22.88) and in order to reach the trench had to take a more circuitous route, their entry into the enemy line was thus retarded.

At this point Lieut. C.H.MAGAHY who was leading the party was wounded and his runner killed.

"D" party took up their position as a covering party. "A" and "C" parties proceeded along the trench mopping up the two shafts of the tunnel met with. A prisoner was taken from each, after persuasion. Sentries were posted over the entrances and "P" bombs were thrown down. On the junction of MARS sap (U.20.b.22.88) and TUNNEL TRENCH being reached a party proceeded down the sap and found the Mebu strongly held, the garrison being apparently 8 to 10. A small party of the enemy detached themselves from the remainder of the garrison and attempted to work towards "A" and "C" party, bombing and firing rifles. Our men retaliated with bombs and revolvers; two men were seen to fall, one being shot at close range by Capt. DENCH, M.C. who was O.C. Party. This caused the party to retire towards the Mebu. It was impossible to approach the bodies as the enemy were covering them with rifle fire and bombs.

(2)

During these operations an R.E. party under Major HOLBROW were making a reconnaissance of the trench (see separate report).

At this time the enemy began to shell his own front line and as touch had not been established between "A" and "B" parties O.C. party decided that an attack on the Mebu itself was impracticable. Shortly afterwards the recall signal was seen and the parties rallied successfully. Parties withdrew under rifle fire from the direction of MARS (U.20.b.22.88) and succeeded in getting back into our own trench at the points of departure without further casualties. Previous to the return two red and two green lamps had been displayed in prominent positions on the flanks in our front line. These materially assisted the withdrawal.

NOTES.

1. All ranks taking part in the raid wore a white armlet on the right arm which proved a successful means of identification.
2. From the outset no machine gun or rifle fire was noticed from JOVE (U.20.b.42.74) or South of this point.
3. Telephones and signalling lamps were brought over with "A" and "B" parties. There was no necessity for their use afterwards. All instruments were brought back. Communications between O.C. Enterprise and Advanced Battn. H.Q. worked excellently.
4. The Medical arrangements were excellent and the excellent work of the Battalion Stretcher Bearers deserves special mention.
5. The gas ruse proved entirely successful. All enemy met were wearing respirators and this probably accounts for the absence of machine gun fire. Prisoners appeared to be in a very demoralized condition.
6. No telephone wires were seen in the enemy trench.

ENEMY'S BARRAGE.

7. This began at Zero plus 5 minutes 45 seconds. It fell between TIGER TRENCH and front line and on BEAUMAN'S SUPPORT, but was not heavy. At Zero plus 12 minutes the barrage increased slightly, slackening down at Zero plus 25 minutes and gradually ceasing.
8. The system of checking return of all parties was as follows:-
All ranks carried in their right trousers pocket a card bearing their number, name and party to which they belonged. These were collected by Straggler's Posts in all communication trenches and returned to Battalion Orderly Room at 4 a.m. A roll call was taken at rendezvous on return of parties. This dual system proved very efficient and at 5 a.m. all were accounted for except one known to be killed.
9. Lieut. MAGAHY's runner was killed approaching the enemy's wire. Stretcher Bearers of this party were at the time occupied in assisting wounded and as the party was advancing towards the enemy trench the body had to be left and unfortunately could not be recovered. (Subsequent patrol failed to find the body). No identification marks were on the man.
10 TUNNEL TRENCH. The trench was from 10 to 12 feet deep, about 12 feet wide at the top tapering to 6 feet at the bottom, trench boards were laid down but the sides were not revetted and were very roughly cut. It was drained into sump holes, and appeared well kept. A latrine built into the side of the parapet and containing two fly-proof boxes were found. Sentry posts built of earth jutted from the parapet after the manner of platforms. Two or three steps led down to the entrances to the stairways into the tunnel. One of the entrances was covered

by a piece of sacking. No gas proof curtains were seen. The stairs descended to what was probably the first landing for about 20 or 30 feet and a fire could be seen burning at the bottom. Entrances were about 50 yards apart.
11 Casualties:-

       Officers .... Two slightly wounded.
               .... One (temporarily incapacitated, returned to duty)

       Other Ranks..... Killed 1
          do   ..... (Slightly
                      (Wounded...4
          do   ..... Wounded
                      remaining
                      on duty. ..1

       Total - Officers and O.Rs ..... 9.

    I hope to bring to your notice later the names of those who especially distinguished themselves.

                                   (sd) G.A.M.BUCKLEY, Lieut. Col.
16-10-17.   Commanding 7th Bn. Leinster Regiment.

WAR DIARY

FOR MONTH OF NOVEMBER, 1917.

VOLUME :- 2H

UNIT :- 7th Leinster Regiment

Army Form C. 2118.

WAR DIARY
of
7th LEINSTER REGT.
INTELLIGENCE SUMMARY.
(Erase heading not required.)

Instructions regarding War Diaries and Intelligence Summaries are contained in F. S. Regs., Part II. and the Staff Manual respectively. Title pages will be prepared in manuscript.

Place	Date	Hour	Summary of Events and Information	Remarks and references to Appendices
DURROW CAMP	Nov.	1st.	Parade Service for R.Cs in the morning. In the afternoon inter- Coy. Coy. competition area held. Bg.D. Coys. hung basketball winners.	
		2nd.	Church Parade in the morning for C of E. Presbyterians & Nonconformists. In the evening the Battalion relieved the 6th CONNAUGHT RANGERS in support sectors. Dispositions — Right Front - B Coy. — D Left " - " - C Right Support - " - A Left " - " - B Butts N.R. TU 25.6.b.2. — 2 Platoons Main Support	
			R.Coy. was complete about 8p.m. a great sight to Coys. as storm ended just before leaving CAMP. 40 dinners. —	
			The following officers joined. — 2/Lt H.A. JINKS 2/Lt L.M.J PEARSON 2/Lt J.W BOYES DANIEL DEVAN ORSTONI 2/Lt B.H. FORREST	

A5834 Wt. W4973/M687 750,000 8/16 D. D. & L. Ltd. Forms/C.2118/13.

Army Form C. 2118.

WAR DIARY
or
INTELLIGENCE SUMMARY.
(Erase heading not required.)

7th LEINSTER REGT.

Place	Date	Hour	Summary of Events and Information	Remarks and references to Appendices
In the line	Nov 3rd		Quiet day on the whole. Nothing of importance to report. About 5.30 pm Boche sent about 50 gas shells to a flank.	
		4th	At about 2.30 am there was a little shelling of our front trenches on our right. Nothing of importance in day time.	
		5th	There was just a little gun bombardment of the Piket on our right accompanied by gun shelling of gun behind left.	
		6th	From 6 am to 11 am 4.2s fell every 3 or 4 minutes nearly on RAILWAY RESERVE. At about 10.30 am R.S.M Clarke was unfortunately killed by a shell whilst entering his dug-out. He was buried the same evening at the ...side. In MAIDA VALE (T24d. 9.1). During the a... No. 11 Post was blown in and destroyed by a 4.2. 6 wounded & about 1 killed & 3 wounded.	
	7th		Quiet day. Nothing to report.	
	8th		Enemy retaliated at noon with some 150cm shells on PELICAN AVENUE. Otherwise a quiet day.	
	9th		On 3rd Bde agent at 10.30 pm & fine 5.30 fell in vicinity of MAIN SUPPORT trench just on our front line during operation San Juan - on our right.	

A5854. Wt. W4973/M687 750,000 8/16 D. D. & L. Ltd. Forms/C.2118/13.

WAR DIARY
or
INTELLIGENCE SUMMARY

Army Form C. 2118

7th LEINSTER REGT.

Place	Date	Hour	Summary of Events and Information	Remarks and references to Appendices
In the Field	Nov. 10th		A very quiet day. Nothing to report.	
	11th		During the afternoon there was intermittent registration on RAILWAY RESERVE. 9/9 Salvoes of target.	
	12th		An unsuccessful Gas & smoke bombardment was carried out at 7.30am against enemy positions in TUNNEL TRENCH.	
	13th		A day of normal activity. One man return shoulder by stray of bullet.	
	14th		Nothing to report.	
	15th		Exchange of HH's bombarded from 11am to 11.45pm enemy front line received UROB with good results.	
	16th		Under the most enterprising circumstances 2nd Lt. G.M.E. GIRARD accidentally met two above officers while on the front line at 7.45 and 5.15 at 1.30pm in the avenue of the above trench. 2nd Lt. F. Rutter 5th M.C. of the C.O. who after and warned others [?] again. Sig. No 5/F.G. the vicinity [?]	
	17th		During afternoon & evening enemy shelled with "5" RAILWAY RESERVE. One direct hit destroyed a dugout resulting 5- casualties.	
	18th		The Battn was relieved at 7.40pm as per attached orders & proceeded to DYSART CAMP arriving 11.55pm Coy R.E. for arranging. 6 men were admitted to 49/F. M.C.	
Dysart Camp	19th		Fatigues 30 men to 49/F.M.G.C. The annual meeting of Parties as part of day were found by the Battn Order No 171. Instructing the am & pm was held at Orderly Room to study side.	
In the Field	20th		An accident with Indian Received the Battn moved off at 7am and took an overland route to DON TRE H.C.M. 70yds east of DON RD. (ref sheet 57cNW5113SW) L. the	

WAR DIARY or INTELLIGENCE SUMMARY

Army Form C.2118.

7th LEINSTER REGT.

Place	Date	Hour	Summary of Events and Information	Remarks and references to Appendices
Nov. In the field	20th		The same working parties & fatigues were found together with 1/150 small ones making a total of 3 fatigues & 145 O.R. and having a hundred men in navigation of DOI TR. These were joined by a party of B.B. Irish in navigation of Adv B bays left to Isol N.G. in RAILWAY RESERVE (a cond. of laying off Adv 8.30am Adv B bays left for a short time at mouth of bays to apply to BURG TR MAHN SUPPORT with a short time at BUHL RD. to MEBUS & bays from apply to MAHN from its junction with BUHL RD. to MEBUS & bays from there to MAHN SUPPORT. The remainder of the Battn. was lifted at 2/70-5am to SUPPORT. The remainder of the Battn. was lifted at 11am to Support under RAILWAY RESERVE at 1st Battn. Hq which was funded at Main of Support under 1.30pm retained by 2 LG teams from C Coy. 2 Lt TRIGG & BEAMAN & parties. 1.30pm retained by 2 LG teams from C Coy. 2 Lt TRIGG & BEAMAN & parties up this work in carrying ammunition mounts. The men 10 marks under heavy fire. Casualties. 8 O.R. wounded of the RZ. using 1 party 2 men were hit by 2 mens on machine bullet - unarmed. The situation during the night was unchanged. at 10am the Battn. commenced regrouping by trails. The ration lorry hinted matters.	
	21st		at 6.30pm the 9/12 Cays arrived & reliever 2 during the night. MANS MARS. finished with MOTH SHP SHY MARS MARE. Casualties: 10 O.R. wounded making a total for the duration of 2 K 17 B w.	
	22nd		at 10 am The Battn. relieved the 6/E Colm. bango up in TUNNEL TR. Battn. Hq moved to QUEENS LANE near H.Q. C. Coy. took the line from MARTIN RR.6 extent at St MARS SAP & D Coy from that to MARS to U4d 18·18. Casualties - 3 O.R. wounded in taking over the lines. Casualties of 2K 176w.	
	23rd		at 10 am Two parties totalling 65 as 1st attached to Machine GO. attached by distant consolidated the nuclei STOVE I TUNNEL TR. to U20 3 5·7. The mineral was blocked by R.E. & a C.T. dug from UJV E to M013 SAP by party of 118. HANDS pioneers. Many [?] there killed & 31 taken prisoner. Considerable might roll was also captured including l min sweep 2 bayonet barrel & 4 L.G. with considerable of ammunition including one L.T. 2 megadyne rockets and classified apparatus.	

[signed] C. Noteum

WAR DIARY or INTELLIGENCE SUMMARY

Army Form C. 2118.

7 Leinster Regt

Place	Date	Hour	Summary of Events and Information	Remarks and references to Appendices
NOV In the field	23rd		Portions of a Listening Patrol missing. 2nd Lts FUDGER & RYAN wounded – Minor Casualties.	
	24th		Bn. quietly held – making a total for the operations of 5 K + 28 wounded. At noon the line into Talyon took up the positions of A, B & C Coys. During the day the dispositions of A, B & C Coys to relieve MANN SUPPORT. The line was now taken over by Brigade. Clearing of TUNNEL TR. was [?] by a patrol of 2 Offrs & 120 O.R. left the line at head of MASSAP to ascertain the FORT RHINE BULLECOURT Rd & VINCAN which were found to be unoccupied. Casualties: 1 OR wounded.	
	25th		Bn quiet day. Cpt. Hm. & patrol left TOVE to reconnoitre TUNNEL TR. & GC to PLUTOI where the wire was found to be [?]. During the day at 11 am in the front line and the Bn. was relieved by 6th R.M.F. at 11am in the front line and moved to STRAY SUPPORT. D Coy. remaining in MANN SUPPORT.	
	26th		Bn. was relieved by 1st R.M.F. & marched to MEPYAL & MAIDA VALE & thence by light railway to DURROW CAMP. Nothing to report.	
DURROW CAMP	27th			
	28th	11 am	Gen. Hickie inspected the Battn. & thanked them for the good work they had done.	
	29th		Nothing to report.	
	30th		Nothing to report.	

S. A. M. Farmer [?]
LIEUT COLONEL
COMMANDING 7th (S) Bn LEINSTER REGIMENT

SECRET AMENDED ORDER NO 5. COPY No. 12

In the Field. 17th November, 1917.

1. Secret Order No 4 is cancelled and the following substituted.

RELIEF. The Battalion, less "A" Coy, will be relieved in the line to-morrow, 18th inst. by the 6th CAMERONI HIGHLANDERS.

3. "A" Coy, less 2 Lewis Gun teams, and personnel for (a) snipers posts in PEREGRIN (b) O.P. in WILCAR will be relieved by 4th ROYAL FUSILIERS.
    O.C. "A" Coy will arrange for guides to be at junction of WILCAR AVENUE and ??????? AVENUE at 5.30. p.m.

4. Two Lewis Gun teams of "A" Coy. and personnel for PEREGRIN and WILCAR posts will be relieved by 6th CAMERONI HIGHLANDERS.

5. The leading Platoon of the 6th CAMERONI HIGHLANDERS will not cross the ??????????????? road before 5 p.m.

6. On relief the Battalion will move to DWYART CAMP and take over the huts etc. occupied by the relieving unit.

7. Completion of relief by front line Companies will be reported to Battalion Head Qrs. in code as follows:-
    "A" Coy Relief by 4th ROYAL FUSILIERS........ WARD.
    "A" & "A" Companies complete relief........... WYORD.
    Companies in reserve will report by runner.

8. TRANSPORT. Necessary arrangements will be made by the Transport Officer for removal of Lewis Guns, Officers Kits, Coy. and Head Qr. Mess gear etc. Officers will arrange with their own Grooms for chargers.

9. ADVANCE PARTIES. 1 Officer, 1 N.C.O. and 1 man. per Coy and Head Qrs. will be at DWYART CAMP by 3 p.m. 18.11.17 to take over and allot accommodation.

10. TRENCH STORES. All trench store lists, signed by relieving unit, will be handed in to Orderly Room by 9 a.m. 19.11.17.
    Having regard to the number of inter-company reliefs that have taken place during this tour, Officers Commanding Companies will please take special care in checking the accuracy of these lists.

11. WORKING PARTIES. The relieving unit will take over all working parties at present found by the Battalion. All information concerning these must be handed over before departure.

12. BATTLE KITS. The Quartermaster will arrange to take over DWYART CAMP prior to the arrival of the Battalion.

13. ACKNOWLEDGE.

John R. M. Phillips
Captain,
Adjutant 7th Battalion Leinster Regt.

Copies to recipients of Secret Order No 4 and O.C. 6th ROYAL FUSILIERS.

JAMES.   SECRET ORDER   NO.4.

RELIEF.   In the Field 17/11/17

1. The Battalion will be relieved in the line by JABBER to-morrow 18??
   On relief the Battalion will proceed to TYBANT CAMP AND TAKE OVER
   the huts etc. vacated by the relieving unit.

2. ADVANCE PARTIES. 1 Officer, 1 N.C.O. and 1 man per Coy and H.Q.
   will be at TYBANT CAMP by 3. p.m. 18. 11.17 to take over and allot
   accommodation.

3. REPORTS. Completion of relief will be reported to present Battalion
   Head Qrs. Front line (Coys) will report by wire (code word TENTH) reserve
   Companies by runner.

4. TRENCH STORES. All trench store lists, signed by relieving unit, will
   be handed in to Orderly Room by 9.a.m. 19.11.17.
   Having regard to the number of inter-company reliefs
   that have taken place during this tour, Officers Commanding Companies
   will please take special care in checking the accuracy of these lists.

5. MESS KITS. Arrangements have been made for a Battalion Officers Mess
   in TYBANT CAMP. Coy. Mess Kits may be dumped in WINRAY DUGOUTS South where
   a guard will be arranged for them till the next tour in the trenches.

6. WORKING PARTIES. The relieving unit will take over all working parties
   at present found by the Battalion. All information concerning these
   must be handed over before departure.

7. TAKING OVER. The Quartermaster will arrange to take over TYBANT CAMP
   prior to the arrival of the Battalion.

8. TRANSPORT. Necessary arrangements for Officers chargers, transport
   of Lewis guns, Officers kits etc. will be made by the Transport
   Officer

9. TIME. Relief may be expected to take place between 5 and 6 p.m.

                                    J.A.M. Pla...
                                             Captain.
                                Adjutant, 7th Battalion Leinster Regt.

Copies to :-
1. Than.   8. Transport Officer.
2. Winner.   9. Jabber.
3. O.C. "A" Coy.   10. Jack.   )
4. O.C. "B"   "   11. Jailer.) For Information.
5. O.C. "C"   "   12. War Diary.
6. O.C. "D"   "   13. File.
7. Quartermaster.   14. Retained.

16th (Irish) Division,
B. E. F.

O.C.

7th Leinster Regiment.

Once more I wish to express to you as Commanding Officer, and to the Officers, Non-commissioned Officers and men of the Battalion my appreciation of the work of the Battalion.

I am glad that it fell to the Leinsters to put the finishing touch to the victory of CROISSILLES Heights by the capture of the enemy's Strong Point in JOVE Mebus. The taking of Jove gave us over 700 yards of enemy's trench, which he had to blow up and evacuate.

Once more I beg you to convey to all ranks of the 7th Leinsters my admiration and my thanks.

(sd) W.B. Hickie Major General,
Commanding 16th (Irish) Division.

November 28th 1917.

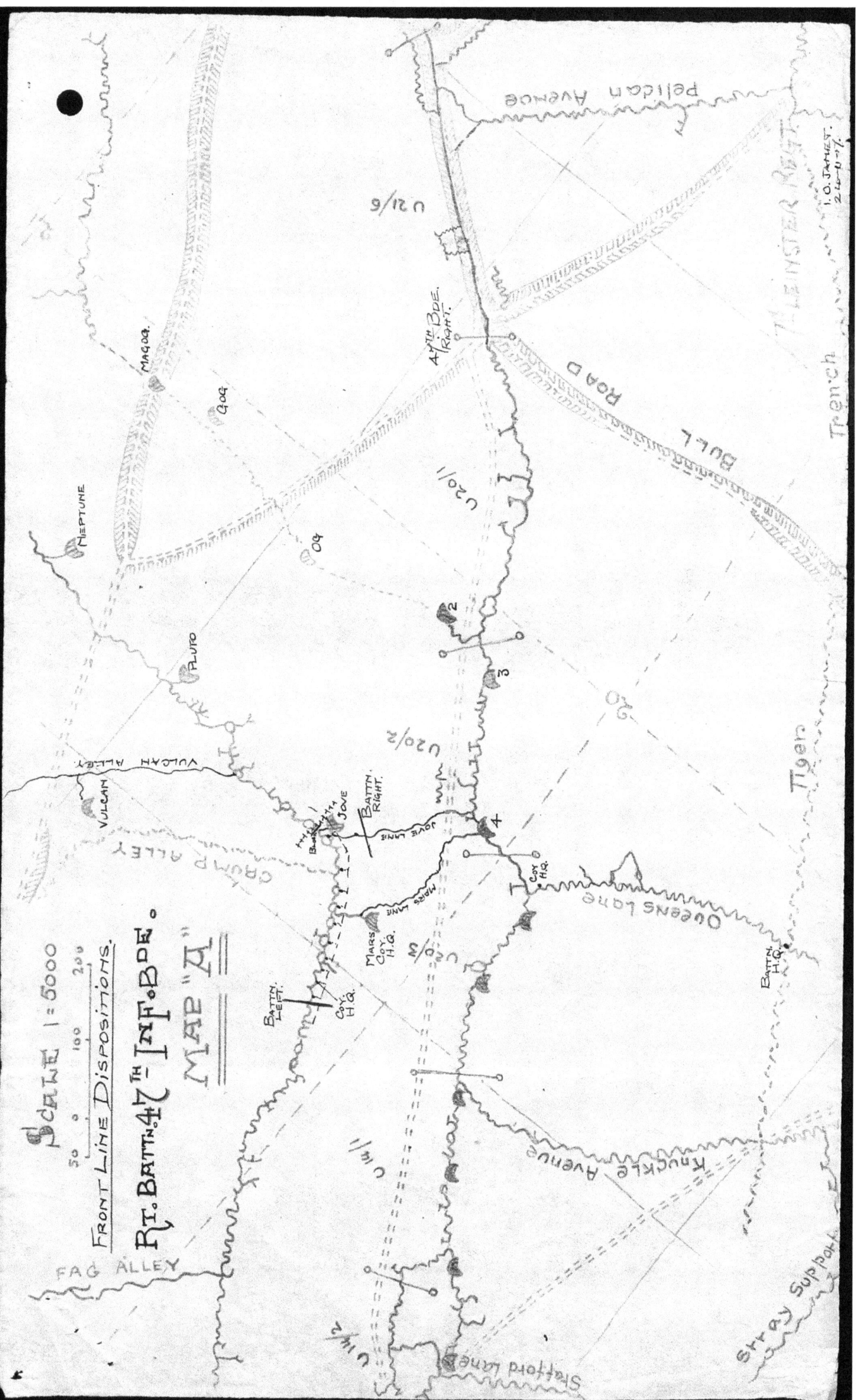

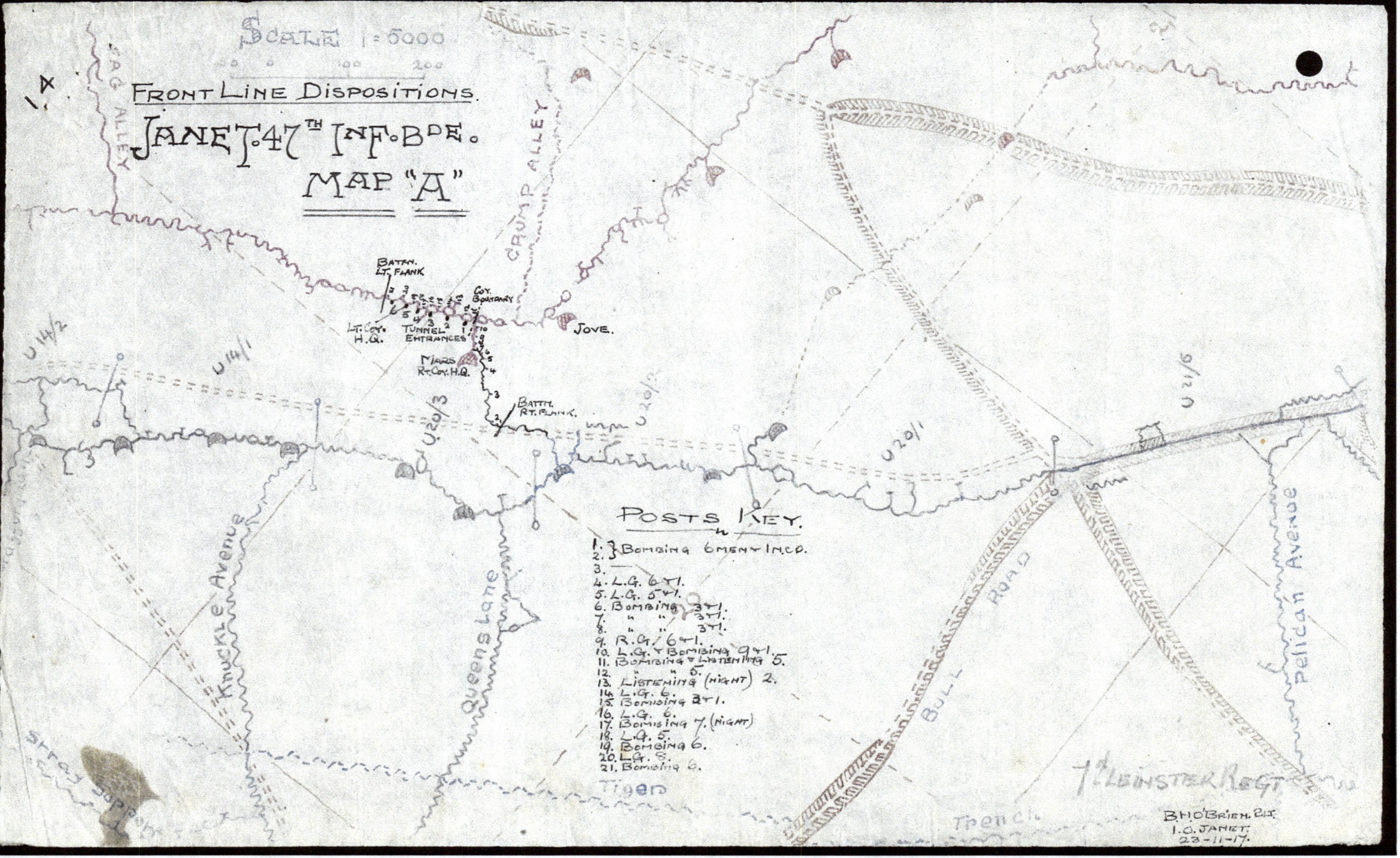

1A
SCALE 1:5000
100
200
FRONT LINE DISPOSITIONS.
JANET. 47TH INF. BDE.
MAP "A"
FAG ALLEY
CRUMP ALLEY
BATTN. LT. FLANK
COY. BOUNDARY
LT. COY. H.Q.
TUNNEL ENTRANCES
JOVE.
MARS RT. COY. H.Q.
BATTN. RT. FLANK.
U 14/2
U 14/1
U 20/3
U 20/1
U 21/6
Knuckle Avenue
Queens Lane
Bull Road
Pelican Avenue
Tiger
Trench
Stray Support
POSTS KEY.
1. 2. Bombing 6 men & I.N.C.O.
3. —
4. L.G. 6 & 1.
5. L.G. 5 & 1.
6. Bombing 3 & 1.
7. " " 3 & 1.
8. " " 3 & 1.
9. R.G. / 6 & 1.
10. L.G. & Bombing 9 & 1.
11. Bombing & Listening 5.
12. " " 5.
13. Listening (night) 2.
14. L.G. 6.
15. Bombing 3 & 1.
16. L.G. 6.
17. Bombing 7. (night)
18. L.G. 5.
19. Bombing 6.
20. L.G. 8.
21. Bombing 6.
1st LEINSTER REGT.
B.H. O'Brien. 2Lt.
I.O. JANET.
23-11-17.

WAR   DIARY,

FOR MONTH OF DECEMBER, 1917.

VOLUME :- 25

UNIT :- 2/10th Leinster Regiment.

Army Form C. 2118.

WAR DIARY
or
INTELLIGENCE SUMMARY.
(Erase heading not required.)

1st LEINSTER REGT.

Place	Date	Hour	Summary of Events and Information	Remarks and references to Appendices
DURROW CAMP.	DEC. 1st		Nothing to report	
	2nd		The Battn. attended church in ERVILLERS during the morning and at 4 p.m. were relieved in the camp by the 12th S.W.B., marching by road to cavalry camp in A28d (57°) near GOMIECOURT	
GOMIECOURT	3rd		Another march was commenced at 12.30 p.m. via SAPIGNIES & BAPAUME to "E" hut camp in H18c(57°) just north of BEAUMONT where the Battn. remained under one hours notice to move.	
BEAULANCOURT	4th		A quiet day in camp.	
	5th		Nothing to report	
	6th		The Battn. moved at 8 a.m. in cap and rest with attached C.O. N.S.11 via bus old through careful march during a fresh and implosion by the day avoided on place. Drivers were asked during a 70 min. half at Bapaume. The journey was finished without incident, the Battn. reaching MOISLAINS.	
TINCOURT.	7th		Nothing to report	
	8th		" " "	
	9th		" " "	
	10th		Line reconnoitred by Coy. Commdrs.	
	11th		The Battn. moved off at 9 a.m. in poor climate with P.O. N° 12, marching by road to St EMILIE where it mot its field kitchens and then proceeded to front line ready to relieve 9 Nov. 2 R.D. Fusiliers was uneventfully completed by 9.30 p.m.	
FRONT LINE.	12th		Day pleasant. Enemies artillery quiet over in a very muddy condition due to recent rains. 15.9 felt 5 yds from H.Q. area causing slight damage.	
	13th			

Army Form C. 2118.

WAR DIARY
or
INTELLIGENCE SUMMARY.
(Erase heading not required.)

Place	Date	Hour	Summary of Events and Information	Remarks and references to Appendices
FRONT LINE	DEC. 13th		Quiet day. During the night a bomb thrower was used of the GILLEMONT FM. POST'S supporters, one man killed.	
	14th		An intensive enemy rifle + M.G. fire at dusk when A Coy the place of C in the left of the front of Bn. The right was relieved by the North'd + D. on the left.	
	15th	9.10 am	Heavy G.W. fell near GILLEMONT POST without effect. During the morning E.A. were very active over the line of the Bn.	
	16th	6.10 am	An artillery party of about 20 strong approached BLUNT NOSE but were quickly dispersed.	
	17th		SOME 13 by the 6th R. Irish Regt. the Batt. who relieved accompanying by 1o/m without incident. And the relief completed quietly. T.M.s were active during the morning. Firing to w/ch enemy T.M. responses. Quiet M.O. POST obtaining 6 direct things omitted again of GILLEMONT POST Retaliation from Stokes T.M. + 4.5" hows.	
STEENWERCK	18th		The Enemy sd. alarmed by retaliation from Stokes T.M. + 4.5" hows. N° 181411E was shelled with 5.9s during the evening of Batn. H.Q. N° 181411E in the early morning by Batn. 3 M.G. went missing. Wire nothing two working parties when found by Bn. at Bde. H.Q. and 1 Officer + 40 men under R.E. building huts in Rly. Cutting filled.	
	19th		In addition to the same working parties as yesterday 1 off + 50 men were despatched to work at Gold M.R. During the morning orders to those of yesterday were found by Batn.	
	20th		The following Officers joined the 15th.— 2nd Lto. H.G. MARKHAM, H. WYLDE, PLAWRENCE, J.M. HUNTER, J.B. TOHER, F.P. MAGUIRE, A. CHAPMAN, A. POLLARD-URQUHART, C.J. HERBERT. Mr. KEATING, D.J.	

Army Form C. 2118

WAR DIARY
or
INTELLIGENCE SUMMARY
(Erase heading not required.)

Instructions regarding War Diaries and Intelligence Summaries are contained in F. S. Regs., Part II. and the Staff Manual respectively. Title Pages will be prepared in manuscript.

Place	Date	Hour	Summary of Events and Information	Remarks and references to Appendices
STEENWJE	Dec. 21st & 22nd		Divided working parties to those of yesterday were found and an addition amount for entering eighth cable.	
TINCOURT	23rd		2nd Lt. I.M. JONES returned from sick leave 22-27. OM. moves the Battn. was blew by 7½ R.I. Res. 20 per attached O.O.N. 14 and reached by 7 am by TINCOURT occupying practically the same billets as on the 5 inst.	
			Nothing to report.	
			The env. was seen t.m. delivering hybrid in the mentioned manner. Nothing to report.	
	24th		" "	
	25th		" "	
	26th			
	27th			
	28th			
IN THE LINE	29th		The Battn. moved off in accordance with attached O.O.15 and travelled by rail to STEENWJE whence it marched by road to E.S. tent where "D" Coy took over the right & "C" the left 1/3 the line arrived at the Reserve dugouts. The relief was completed without everyday by 7.30pm. approx a coming party of 1 platoon was found by "D" Coy for a coming party of the 1/8 HANTS. about 8.30 pm the battn. transport was shelled at X roads in F.6a wounding one man & causing damage to 1 vehicle. Otherwise a quiet night. The following officers reported fit for duty: Lt. J.K.B. BAILEY. 2Lt. W.B. TOOLAN.	

Army Form C. 2118

WAR DIARY
or
INTELLIGENCE SUMMARY
(Erase heading not required.)

Place	Date	Hour	Summary of Events and Information	Remarks and references to Appendices
FRONT LINE	Dec. 30. 31st		Quiet day - nothing to report. 13 Coy. found working party of 4 men & 2 am to 6 am. very heavy bombardment by Maj. Bean H2 and (B45) Corps 12 and front line. collection of shells recd. and/indicating 380 shells. Damage insignificant. "B" Coy. found working parties of 11 at 8 pm + Whn. for building shelters off the main road entirely Ms. o speed. fire along the front for a few minutes.	

G.a.m. Buckley, LIEUT COLONEL.
COMMANDING, 7TH (S) BN. LEINSTER REGIMENT (R.C.)

No. 11. ## OPERATION ORDERS

Copy No. 12

by
Lieut. Col. G.A.M. BUCKLEY, D.S.O.
Commanding 7TH Leinster Regt.

1. The Battalion will march from BEAULENCOURT to TINCOURT to-morrow Dec. 8TH., parade at 8.45.a.m.

2. Route ROCQUIGNY---MANANCOURT---MOISLAINS---TEMPLEUX-la-FOSSE.

3. The Battalion will pass Brigade starting point (N.24.d.1.9) at 9.10. a.m. when the Brigadier will inspect Units.

4. Steel Helmets will be worn by all ranks.

5. Advance party of 1.N.C.O. per Coy.Headquarters and Transport will report to Lieut G. FARRELL at 6. p.m. to-night for instructions.

6. Order of March. Headquarters, "D", "A", "B" "C" Coy's, Attached Units, Transport.

7. Strict march discipline will be observed.

8. Coy Officers will be careful to see that all men are turned out according to Regimental pattern shown yesterday.

8. The Camp must be left scrupulously clean and a certificate to this effect from each Coy handed to the Adjutant on parade.

9. Blankets will be stacked in rolls of 10 at 8 a.m. Officers Kits and Mess Kits at 8.15.a.m.

10. Arrival in new Billets will be repoted by Runner to Bn.Hd.Qrs.

(sd) A.H. Whitehead.Captain,
Adjt 7th Leinster Regiment.

Copy No 1 to C.O.
.. No 2 to 2nd in Command.
.. ..3 to Adjt.
.. ..4 to O.C. "A" Coy.
.. ..5 O.C. "B" ..
.. ..6 O.C. "C" ..
.. ..7 O.C. "D" ..

Copy No 8 Transport Officer
.. .. 9 Quartermaster
.. .. 10. Signalling Officer.
.. .. 11. 47th Inf Bde.
.. .. 12 War Diary.
.. .. 13 Retained.

and EAST of that place of platoons at 500x interval.

OPERATION ORDERS No. 13. Copy No ..../2

by
Lieut. COLONEL G.A.M. Buckley D.S.O.
Commanding Janet.
In the Field 16th December, 1917.

---

1. The Bn. will be relieved in the right sub-section by the 6th R.Irish Regt. to-morrow Decr.17th.
2. On relief the Bn will proceed to ST EMILIE dispositions as follows:-
   "A" "B" "C" "D" Coy' In RLY Cutting E. 23.d.
   Head Qrs at E. 24. a.3.1.
3. Advance parties of 1 Officer per Coy will proceed to St EMILIE to take over shelters arriving at 2 p.m. C.Q.M.Sgts will meet the advance party at the shelters.
   Capt J.N.M. Staniforth will take over Headqrs
4. A guide will meet No 1's of Lewis Gun Teams of R.Ir.Regt at X roads F. 21.c 3.9. at 11 a.m. and bring them to DUNCAN POST where a guide from each team of "A" and "B" Coy's will bring them to front line at 12 noon.
5. 4 Guides will meet incoming L.G. Teams at 2.30 p.m. at F. 21. c.3.9. and bring them to DUNCAN POST where their own No 1's will meet them.
6. 1 Guide per Platoon and 2 for Headqrs.will meet incoming unit at X roads F. 16 c. 0.1. at 5.p.m. Guides will be in charge of 2nd Lieut O'Brien and meet him at Bn. Hd. Qrs(Guides in pars 4 and 5 will be Scouts)
7. Trench stores, Maps, Defence schemes etc. will be handed over on relief and a certificate of cleanliness obtained
   Trench store lists and certificates to be at O.Room by 10 a.m. December 18th.
8. Completion of relief to be reported to Bn.Hd.QrsKEYLANE the code word "SNOWBALL" being used.

9. Transport
   Lewis Gun Limbers at DUNCAN POST at 5.p.m.
   Mess cart 5.p.m. at .. .. for
   Coy Mess kit calling at Bn.Hd.Qrs 5.30.p.m.
   Limber for Officers Kits at Bn.Hd.Qrs 5.30.p.m
   Maltese cart at DUNCAN POST at 5.30.p.m.

   (sd) A.H. Whitehead Capt.
   Minnow Janet.

Coy No 1 to C.O.
.. 2. O.C. "A" Coy.
.. 3 O.C "B"
.. 4 O.C "C" ..
.. 5 O.C "D" ..
.. 6. Qr.Mr.
.. 7 Tpt Officer.
.. 8 R.Ir. Regt.
.. 9 47th bde.
..10. Intelligence Officer.
.. 11 R.S.M.
.. 12 War Diary.

OPERATION ORDERS   No 14.
                    By   Copy No......
        Lieut.Colonel G.A.M. Buckley, D.S.O.
        Commanding 7th Battalion Leinster Regiment.

                                In the Field. 22nd December,1917.
        ==

1.   The Battalion will be relieved in Brigade Reserve by 7/8th
        Royal Irish Fusiliers, to-morrow December 23rd, at Noon.

2.   The Battalion on relief will march to HAMEL and occupy the
        same billets as vacated on 10th December.

3.   Route. ROISEL-HAM UADE- All movement will be by Companies
        at 800 yards interval.

4.   Advance parties of 1 Officer and 1 N.C.O. per Company and
        Headquarters will report to Lieut. FARRELL at 9.30.a.m. at
        Orderly Room.

5.   Area stores will be handed over to incoming unit and receipts
        obtained. Companies will obtain certificates for the clean and
        sanitary condition of lines handed over, same to be forwarded to
        O.Room by 10.a.m. 24th inst.

6.   Blankets will be rolled neatly in bundles of 10 and stacked
        near road by 10.a.m.- Officers kits and mess gear to be ready
        at 11.a.m.

7.   Transport will move independently of the Battalion.

8.   O.C. Companies will report arrival in billets to Battn. Head-
        quarters.

                                (sd) A.H. Whitehead Captain,
                                     Adjt 7th Bn. Leinster Regt.

        Copy No 1 to C.O.
             "   2 .. 2nd in Command.
             "   3 .. 47th Inf. Bde.
             "   4... 7/8th R.Ir.Fus.
             "   5 .. O.C. "A" Coy.
             "   6. O.C. "B"   "
             "   7. O.C. "C"   "
             "   8. O.C. "D"   "
             "   9. Transport Officer.
             " 10. Quartermaster.
             " 11. Lieut Farrell.
             " 12. R.S.M.
             " 13. War Diary.
             " 14. File.

Operation Orders No. 15.
By Copy No. 14.
Lieut Colonel G.A.M. Buckley, D.S.O.
Commanding 7th Battalion Leinster Regiment.
In the Field, 28th December, 1917.

----

1. The 7th LEINSTER REGIMENT will relieve the 10th ROYAL DUBLIN FUSILIERS in the front line(left sub-section) to-morrow 29th inst.

2. On completion of relief the disposition of the Battalion will be as follows :-
Battalion Headquarters......... S.1. d. 70.80.
"A" Coy..................... Reserve Coy.
"B" " .... Support Coy.
"C" " .... Left Coy.
"D" " .... Right Coy.

3. The Battalion will parade at TINCOURT siding at 3.30.p.m. whence it will be conveyed by train as far as ST. EMILIE.

4. Guides from the 10th Royal Dublin Fusiliers will be at x road T.3.a. 6.3. at 5.30.p.m.

5. There will be no movement E of the EPEHY-LEMPIRE road before 5.30.p.m. Movement after detraining will be by Platoons at 300 yards interval.

6. Advance parties composed of 1 Officer, 1 N.C.O. and one man per Coy, Head Qrs and Battalion Observers will report at Bn Head Qrs 10th R.D.Fus at 1.p.m.
The same precautions will be observed by these parties when under observation from the enemy as by larger bodies of troops.

7. Defence schemes and sketch maps will be taken over, but not aerial photographs. Trench stores and work in hand will be taken over in writing. Copies of same will reach Battalion Head Qrs at 10 a.m. December 30th.

8. Completion of relief will be reported to Battalion Head Qrs without delay, the name of the Company Commander being used as a code word.

9. Relief of Lewis Guns will be carried out independently of the Battalion as follows:-
L.G. Limbers and teams under 1 N.C.O. per Coy,will accompany the advance party as far as Bettn Hd. Qrs. They will remain there while the N.C.O. proceeds to reconnoitre positions Under his direction teams will then carry up their guns as soon as visibility permits. All guns will be in position before the arrival of the main body.

10. Company dixies etc. may be sent up on the L.G. Limbers.

11. Packs and blankets will be stacked at such place as the Qr, Mr may appoint by 12 noon.

12. Officers kits and Mess gear. Officers kits will be collected at 9 a.m. and mess gear at 9 p.m. in the following order:-
"A" "B" "C" and "D" Head Qrs.

13. Present billets will be left in a scrupously clean condition and certificates to this effect will be rendered to Orderly Room before departure.

(sd) J.H.M. Staniforth Captain.
Adjt 7th Bn. Leinster Regiment.

Copies to
1. C.O.
2. 2nd in Command.
3. Adjutant.
4. O.C. "A" Coy.
5. O.C. "B" "
6. O.C. "C" "
7. O.C. "D" "
8. Quartermaster.
9. Transport Officer.
10. Signal Officer.
11. R.S.M.
12. 47th Inf Bde.
13. O.C. 10th R.D.Fus.
14. WAR DIARY.

WAR DIARY

FOR MONTH OF JANUARY, 1918.

VOLUME :- 26

UNIT :- 2/10th Leinster Regiment.

Army Form C. 2118.

WAR DIARY
or
INTELLIGENCE SUMMARY.
(Erase heading not required.)

7/ LEINSTER REGT

Place	Date	Hour	Summary of Events and Information	Remarks and references to Appendices
1918 FRONT LINE	JAN 1st		Ordinary party of 1 Offr & 7 men was found by "C" Coy. Enemy's Wiring party while wiring on Left Coy front. We MONTS while wiring on Left Coy front. Four working parties of 1 NCO & 10 men were engaged in burying cables. Enemy shell sent causing wounds to 2 men. Covering parties of 1 Offr & men were found by "D" & "B" Coys for working party.	
	2nd		Enemy trench mortars were reportedly active. Left "A" Coy being over the night "B" "C" "D" the support "D" the reserve trenches. Inaugurating duties with 6 Tues of yesterday. Lieut Jones Off Morris fell in MULETR wounding Runner & Kavan Gen. between 8.10am & 12.30am about 30 rds of 4.2" mini Bn HQ. From 4.15am & 4.25am a slight barrage only drew on MULETR trenches wounding 7 soldiers of parties of three of yesterday were found by the Births.	
	3rd		The Bn was relieved at night by 6/RIR Regt commanded and taken to P.B 17 by the ordinary traval of the wounded 7 men	

Army Form C. 2118.

WAR DIARY
or
INTELLIGENCE SUMMARY.
(Erase heading not required.)

Instructions regarding War Diaries and Intelligence Summaries are contained in F. S. Regs., Part II. and the Staff Manual respectively. Title pages will be prepared in manuscript.

Place	Date	Hour	Summary of Events and Information	Remarks and references to Appendices
Bn. Sect. HT.	5th		Ridge Reserve M. Centre & S. forming this Bn. supplied working party. 22.N.17.	
Ridge Reserve			The Battn. spent working parties totalling 5 N.C.O. & 87 men for degrees' obstructions. Snow and rain commenced. Myself at Fze 1.6.	
	6th		Working parties similar to those of yesterday were found.	
	7th		" "	
		5th		
			An enter coy. relief was carried out which moved every 6 platoons would be by 4.30pm. "A" coy changed places with "D" & "B" with "C"	
	8th–9th		Working parties were told as before. Was a trench 30 yds long was dug after dark near S.D. & B. Coys at the western edge of ENFER WOOD. During the night J. MARASSISE F.M. and environs LH.	
	9th			
	10th	1.30 pm	the Battn. was relieved by the 4th R.I. Rs. and proceeded	
TINCOURT (Rue Nord)			by march route S.E. S.E. EMILIE where it entrained for TINCOURT. The Same billets were occupied as on the two previous mornings.	
	11th		The day was spent in changing up, baths + kit etc.	
	12th		The Battn. went into training on the lines of that the programme	

Army Form C. 2118.

WAR DIARY
or
INTELLIGENCE SUMMARY.
(Erase heading not required.)

Place	Date	Hour	Summary of Events and Information	Remarks and references to Appendices
TITTCOURT	JAN. 13th		Lt.-Col. G.A.M. BUCKLEY D.S.O. who had been ill went to Hospital relinquishing the command of the Battn. to Capt. V.J. FARRELL M.C.	
	14th		A draft party of 105 men & [?] joined the Battn about half way between St Emilie & TINCOURT. The remainder of the Battn also joined as per attached programme. Training as per programme.	
	15th		" " " "	
	16th		" " " "	
	17th		" " " "	
	18th		The Battn. training was continued.	
	19th		" " " "	
	20th		" " " " Landed went to Church in TINCOURT as per attached O.N.? Afternoon the 2nd Battn LEINSTER REGT arrived on a visit from their camp near by. The afternoon & evening we spent in Sports, Hockey, Tug-o-war, Boxing etc. O.C. Staff of 1 M.O. + 16 men [joined?]/[fem?] Base. Battn training continued	
	21st			
	22nd		The Battn. arrived at 91.4pm entrained at HAMEL SIDING and proceeded to	

Army Form C. 2118.

WAR DIARY
or
INTELLIGENCE SUMMARY.
(Erase heading not required.)

Instructions regarding War Diaries and Intelligence Summaries are contained in F. S. Regs., Part II. and the Staff Manual respectively. Title pages will be prepared in manuscript.

Place	Date	Hour	Summary of Events and Information	Remarks and references to Appendices
IN LINE	JAN. 22nd		At ST EMILIE. Here the march route was commenced across country to LEMPIRE and on to front line, the relief being completed without incident at 8.23pm. The disposition of Battn were detailed on Att N°15.	
	23rd		The relief was covered by a party of 1 Off & 20 O.Rs. Found returning to	
	24th		Work was commenced on clearing of front line & C.Ts.	
	24th		Clearing up was carried on all day on water, C.T., relief T.Ts.	
			Place, & changing places with "C" Coy. & "B" with "D". 2nd Lt J.C. LODDER of the 26th INF. REGT. American army was attached to Battn for instruction	
	25th		At 12 midnt a patrol 2 I.Offs & 4 O.Rs of the Right Coy. left front line on NIGHT RAY. reconnoitered BANK in TERRA to enemy listening post but	
			there was found no one were any of that signs of the enemy. The Patrol returned at 2am & reports the TERRA & Bl. news ignited & unmolested.	
	26th		Observing Enemy party of Miss E. Battn attn. am a few of enemy approached the wire C.T. wolf was carried but during the early morning the dispositions being the same as given at the 23rd inst. The Batt was gradually	
	27th		Of very quiet day. Every Lt.Offs between 3.10 am & 4.30am a patrol All 1Off & 5 O.Rs from left Coy. explored No-Mans-Land no PBC. Quiring & thick	

(A/883) D. D. & L.td, London B.C. Wt. W8oq/M1072 350,000 4/17 Sch. 82a. Forms/C/2118/14

WAR DIARY or INTELLIGENCE SUMMARY

Army Form C. 2118.

Place	Date	Hour	Summary of Events and Information	Remarks and references to Appendices
IN LINE	Jan 27th		A daylight reconnaissance of enemy wire was accomplished by Col. AUSTEY. Snowman & the 2nd Lt McCoy	
	28th		Between 2am & 4am a patrol 1 Offr. & 1 NCO replied No-Mans-Land in A/2 B.M. of GILLEMONT FARM. By 8.30 the Batn. was relieved by 6th R.I. Bn. relief attached O.O. No. 16 and marched via ROISEL to Bde. RESERVE at ST EMILIE where Major MATHER who had just returned from leave took over the command.	
ST EMILIE	29th		The day was spent in cleaning. Working party 1 Offr. & 20 men was detailed at 5pm for D.T.M.O. in front of our system.	
	30th		The C.O. inspected "B" Coy at 11am & "C" Coy at 3pm. No F.M.O. occurred nothing heavy to report. Yesterday's D.T.M.O. French	
	31st		1 N.C.O. & 18 men granted French leave. Yesterday's working party was injected.	

D. Mather Lt Col
Comdg. 1st Leinster Regt.

Battalion Orders   No 3.
By
Lieut Colonel G.A.M. Buckley, D.S.O.
Commanding 7th Battalion Leinster Regiment.
In the Field. 12th January, 1918.

---

1. **ROUTINE.** Orderly Room will be at 10.a.m. to-morrow.
   The sick will parade at 9.a.m.

2. **LECTURE** Captain Fish, 22nd Wing, Royal Flying Corps, will give lectures, illustrated with lantern slides, on the various types of aeroplanes and the work of the Royal Flying Corps. The lectures will be given in the Theatre at HAMEL on the 9th, 14th and 23rd inst. commencing at 3.30.p.m.
   These lectures are especially intended for Junior Officers and N.C.O's and it is hoped that as many as possible will attend.

3. **DIVINE SERVICE.** Parade for Divine Service to-morrow will be as follows:-
   Church of England.
   8. a.m. Holy Communion. In Church Army Chapel, Billet 7 TINCOURT.
   11 a.m. Morning Prayer, followed by Holy Communion. In V.M.C.A. Hut.
   Parade at 10.45.a.m.
   6.30. Evening Prayer. In Church Army Hut.
   Presbyterians and Non-Conformist.
   10.a.m.   V.M.C.A. Hut. TINCOURT.
   Parade at 9.45. a.m.
   Roman Catholics.

   10.a.m.   Mass. R.C. Church TINCOURT.
   Parade 9.30.a.m.
   All Officers not on duty will attend.

4. **HORSES.** All clipped horses will be rugged up by day and night when standing in the lines. Unclipped horses will be rugged up by night. Rugs will invariably be carried in all Horse Drawn Vehicles during cold weather and thrown over horses when standing.(V11C.R.O.1233)
   (sd A.H. Whitehead Captain,
   Adjutant 7th Battalion Leinster Reg

7TH (S) BATTALION, THE LEINSTER REGIMENT.
oooooo o ooooooo

AMENDED TRAINING PROGRAMME: January 12th to 14th, 1918.

Times.	January 12th.	January 13th	January 14th.
7.15 a.m.	Muster parade.		Muster parade.
9. to 9.45 a.m	Bayonet Fighting & Physical training.	Church Parade.	Bayonet Fighting & Physical Training.
10 to 10.45.	Squad Drill.	Church parade.	Platoon drill.
11 to 11.45 a.m	Musketry. L.G. Teams.) L.G. Drill.)	Musketry.	Musketry. 2 companies on range until 1.p.m.
11.45 to 12.30.	Arms Drill	Musketry.	Arms Drill (2 Coys)
2 to 4.0 p.m.	Organised Games.	Organised Games.	Organised Games.

11th January, 1918.

Lieut.Colonel.
Commanding 7th (S) Battn. The Leinster Rgt.

SECRET.   7th Leinster Regiment.Order. No. 18. Copy. No......
                                              9th January, 1918.
Ref. Map:- LEMPIRE (Special sheet).
_____

1. The 7TH LEINSTER REGIMENT will be relieved in Brigade
   Support by the 7/8TH ROYAL IRISH FUSILIERS, tomorrow. 10th inst.

2. On completion of relief, the Battalion will proceed by
   march route to ST. EMILIE, thence by train to HAMEL.

3. "A" Coy. 7th Leinsters will be relieved by "D" Coy 7/8 R.
                                                      Irish Fus
   "B" "   "   "   "   "   "   "   "C" "   "   "
   "C" "   "   "   "   "   "   "   "B" "   "   "
   "D" "   "   "   "   "   "   "   "A" "   "   "

4. All Companies will arrange to have guides at the Light
   Rly. crossing, F 8 c 2-8, at 5.30 p.m. They will report
   to 2nd LIEUT. TOHER who will be responsible that they are
   detailed to the correct platoon (3 guides per company, &
   2 for Battn. H.Q.)

5. The following will be handed over, and receipts obtained.
              (a)   All trench stores.
              (b)   Written Defence Scheme.
              (c)   All work in progress, and proposed.
                                      (in writing)
   Receipts to reach Orderly Room by 10.0 a.m., 11th inst,.

6. Advance parties of 7/8th R.I. Fusiliers will report to
   Companies during the forenoon.

7. Movement will be by platoons at 500 yards' interval.

8. Completion of relief will be wired to B. H. Q. in code
   using name of Company Commander.

9. On completion of relief, Companies will march independently to ST. EMILIE SIDING (F.13 c 2-5) where they will
   entrain under orders from the Entraining Officer.

10. On arrival at HAMEL, Battalion Headquarters will be at
    K.19 a 2-9.

11. The Quartermaster will arrange to take over billets in

11. (contd.)

HAMEL.   The usual advance parties will report there at 3.0 p.m. and will meet their respective companies on detrainment at HAMEL Siding.

12.   The Quartermaster will arrange:-
    (i) That an issue of rum be handed over to Company Commanders at ST. EMILIE Siding for issue to men before entraining.
    (ii) That a hot meal is ready on arrival at HAMEL.

13.   The Transport Officer will arrange to have the necessary transport at Company H.Q's as soon as visibility permits.

14.   ACKNOWLEDGE.

                (sd) J. H. M. Staniforth,   Captain.
           Adjutant, 7th Battn. The Leinster Rgt.

Copies to :-

1. C.O,.
2. 2nd in Cmd,.
3. Adjutant.
4. O.C., A. Coy,.
5. " B. "
6. " C. "
7. " D. "
8. Q.M. & T.O.
9. R.S.M.
10. 47th I. Bde.
11. 7/8th R.I. Fus,.
12. 2nd Lt. J. E. TOHER.
13. War Diary.
14. Retained.

7th LEINSTER REGIMENT.

PROGRAMME OF WORK, January 14th to 17th.

TIME.	Jan. 14th.	Jan. 15th.	Jan. 16th.	Jan. 17th.
7.15 a.m.	Muster parade.	Muster parade. (Bayonet fighting and Phys. Trng.)	Muster parade. Bayonet Ftg. & Phys. Trng.	Muster parade. Bayonet Ftg. & Phys. Trng.
9.0 to 9.45 a.m.	MUSKETRY on 300 Yds. Range.			
10.0 to 10.45 a.m.	For all men not on working Parties.	Platoon Drill.	Company Drill.	Company Drill.
11.0 to 11.45 a.m.		Musketry.	Gas Drill.	Route March.
11.45 to 12.30 a.m.		Arms Drill & Guards.	March Discipline	
2.0 to 4.0 p.m.	O R G A N I S E D G A M E S .			

N.B:- The above Programme will be amended by Companies in respect of the times allotted for Range Practice.

SECRET.   Copy. 12

OPERATION ORDERS   NO. 15.

by/ Capt. V. J. Farrell, D.S.
         Commdg. 7th Battn. Leinster Regiment.

In the Field.   ..   ..   21.1.18.
----

1. THE Battalion will relieve the 1st ROYAL DUBLIN FUSILIERS in the Right sub-section on evening of 22nd instant.

2. ON completion, the disposition of the Battalion will be as follows:-
      D. Coy.   Front line (left) - relieving X Coy. R.D.F.
      C. "   "   (right)-   "   Y "   "
      A. "   Support. DUNCAN POST.   "   Z "   "
      B. "   Reserve, KEN LAKE.
      Bn. H. Qrs. KEN LAKE. (F 17a, 3-1.)

3. THE Battalion will entrain at BARRL SIDING at 4.10 p.m. in above order and detrain at ST. EMILIE, proceeding by following route: Cross-country track from Station to F. 14 b, 2-2., thence road to F 15 a, 5.5., F 15 c, 6-1., and F 16 d, 5-3., marching by platoons at 200 yds' intervals

4. GUIDES - Two per Coy, and one for H.Qrs., will meet the Battalion at X Rds., F 16 d, 5-3 at 6.15 p.m.

5. ADVANCE PARTIES, consisting of One Officer, 1 Senior N.C.O. 4 Lewis-Gun No. 1's, Gas N.C.O. per coy., and Intelligence Officer, Signals Sergeant, 1 Lineaman, and 1 N.C.O. from Bn. H.Qrs. will proceed to take over. (Transport arrangements for the party will be notified later)

6. THE following will be taken over:- (a) Trench Stores, (b) written Defence Scheme (c) all documents connected with the line (except air photos) (d) all work in progress and proposed (in writing); Trench Stores lists to be at Orderly Room by 10.0 a.m. 23rd instant.

7. TRANSPORT. Officers' kits, Mess gear, Company Stores, &c. will be collected at 2.0 p.m.
   Lewis Gun limbers will meet the Battalion at ST. EMILIE STATION at 5.0 p.m. where they will be loaded up and proceed to F 16, d, 5-3, where they will meet teams.

8. BILLETS will be left in a scrupulously clean condition and handed over to incoming unit by the Quartermaster. Company Commanders will render a certificate to the Orderly Room that billets have been left in a clean and sanitary state.

9. COMPLETION of relief to be reported to B.H.Q. by code word "ENAN"

                                                       (signed) Capt & Adjt.
                                                       7th Battn. Leinster Regt.

COPIES TO:-

    1. Commdg. Officer.   8.
    2. Adjutant.   8. Transport Officer.
    3. O.C. "A" Coy.   9. Signals
    4. " "B" "   10. 47th Inf. Bde.
    5. " "C" "   11. 1st Royal Dublin Fusiliers.
    6. " "D" "   12. War Diary.
    7. Quartermaster.   13. Retained.

SECRET.

OPERATION ORDERS.   NO. 16.

– by –

Capt. V. J. Worrell, M.C.
Comdg. 7th LEINSTER REGIMENT.
In the Field.. 27 Jany, 1918.

1. THE Battalion will be relieved in the right Sub-section by the 6th ROYAL IRISH REGIMENT, on 28th January.

2. ON relief, the Battalion will proceed to Brigade Reserve in ST. EMILIE. Disposition will be as follows:-

    A, B, C, D, Coys:- in Fly Cutting at N 23 d...
    Headquarters at N 24 a, 8.1.

3. THE Shelters at ST. EMILIE will be taken over by the Quartermaster, 2nd Lt. IRWIN will take over for Headquarters. C.Q.M. Sgts. will meet their Companies on arrival.

4. GUIDES:-
    (a) One Guide per Company will meet incoming Lewis Gun Teams at CRUCIFIX, N 16 c, 1.3., at 6.0 p.m.
    (b) Two Guides per company, and one for Headquarters, will report to 2nd Lt. GUYNN, at Battalion Headquarters, HEN LANE, at 4.30 p.m., and proceed to meet incoming unit at N 16 c, 4.3.

5. TRENCH Stores, Written Defence Schemes, Work in progress & Trespass, will be handed over on relief, and a Certificate of Cleanliness obtained. Trench Store Lists, and Certificates, to be at urgently here by 10.0 a.m. 28th instant.

6. TRANSPORT. Lewis Gun Limbers, Spring Cart, Maltese Cart, to be at DUNCAN POST at 6.0 p.m; Mess Cart and One Limber to be at HEN LANE at 6.0 p.m; Company Mess Gear to be at DUNCAN POST to meet Spring Cart.

7. COMPLETION OF RELIEF to be reported to Battalion Headquarters by Code Word "ABLE". Arrival in Billets to be immediately reported by Runner to Headquarters.

                                        (Sd.) A. H. WHITNEVAL.
                                                Capt & Adjt.
                                                7th Leinster Regiment.

Copies to:- 1. Commdg. Officer.   8. Transport Officer.
             2. Adjutant.   9. Signals
             3. O.C. "A" Coy.   10. 47th Inf. Bde.
             4. "   "B" "   11. 6th Royal Irish Regt.
             5. "   "C" "   12. War Diary.
             6. "   "D" "   13. Retained.
             7. Quartermaster.

SECRET.   7th Leinster Order   No 17. Copy No......

1. The 7th LEINSTERS will be relieved in the left subsection by the 6th 6th ROYAL IRISH REGT. to-morrow, 4th inst.
2. On relief the Battalion will go into Brigade Support and occupy the positions vacated by the relieving unit.
3. Company reliefs will be as follows:-
   "A" Coy 7th Leinsters will be relieved by "B" 6th R.Ir.Regt.
   "B" "   "   "   "   "   " "D" "   "   "
   "C" "   "   "   "   "   " "A" "   "   "
   "D" "   "   "   "   "   " "C" "   "   "

   Each Company will then proceed to the position vacated by its own relief.
4. On completion of relief the Battalion will be disposed as follows:-
   Battalion Headquarters .P. 15.a. 15.30.(LEMPIRE)
   "A" Coy. LEMPIRE, EDEN WOOD, and M V COPSE.
   "B" "   MALASSISE FARM and OLD COPSE.
   "C" "   Cutting in F. 2.c.
   "D" "   Posts in F. 2.a.
5. Guides from "A" Coy will meet their relief at Junction OCKENDEN TRENCH-MALASSISE ROAD. at 5.45.p.m. Guides from "B" Coy will meet their relief at "D" Coy Head Qrs(TETARD TRENCH) at 5.30.p.m. Guides from "C" Coy will proceed to the Head Qrs "A" Coy, 6th Royal Irish Regiment at F.2.a.2.5. at 6.p.m. No guides will be required from "D" Coy.
6. All work on hand and proposed will be handed over in writing. Working parties will continue normally on day of relief. The change in responsibility for these will take place at 6 p.m.
7. Trench store lists will reach Battalion Head Qrs by 10 a.m. 5. 1. 18.
8. Rations, *Packs & Blankets* to-morrow will not be brought up till completion of relief. For the future they will use the ST. EMILIE-ROUSSOY ROAD arriving in turn at LEMPIRE, MALASSISE FARM, and "C" Coy's new Head Qrs.
9. The usual advance parties will report at new positions by 3 p.m. and take over dispositions etc.
10. The Transport Officer will arrange for all Lewis Gun Limbers and necessary transport to be at Battalion Head Quarters by 5.30 p.m. less those for "A" Coy, which will report at that Coy. Head Qrs. at 6 p.m.
11. Completion of relief to be wired to present Battalion Head Quarters using name of Coy. Commander as code

(sd). J.W.M. Staniforth Captain,
Adjutant 7th Bn. Leinster Regt.

Copies to:-
   1. C.O.
   2. Adjutant.
   3. O.C. "A" Coy.
   4. O.C. "B" "
   5. O.C. "C" "
   6. O.C. "D" "
   7. Signal Officer.
   8. Quarter Master.
   9. Transport Officer.
   10. Regtl. Sgt. Major.
   11. O.C. 6th R. Irish Regt.
   12. War Diary.
   13. 47th Inf. Bde.
   14. Retained.

S E C R E T

NOT TO BE TAKEN
FURTHER FORWARD
THAN BATTALION H.Q.

REORGANISATION OF INFANTRY BRIGADES.

16th. Div. No. A/297/G.N/1.

1. Instructions have been received from G.H.Q. that the number of Infantry Battalions in an Infantry Brigade are to be reduced to three. Certain Battalions as stated hereafter will be received by the Division, and certain others broken up.

2. They are as follows :-

To be received.	To be broken up.
2nd. R. Munster Fusiliers.	6th. R. Irish Regiment.
2nd. Leinster Regiment.	8/9th. R. Dublin Fusiliers.
	10th. R. Dublin Fusiliers.
	7/8th. R. Irish Fusiliers.
	7th. Leinster Regt.

3. On completion of reorganisation the "Order of Battle" of Inf. Brigades will be as follows :-

47th. Inf. Bde.	48th. Inf. Bde.	49th. Inf. Bde.
6th. Connaught Rgrs.	1st. R. Dublin Fus.	2nd. R. Irish Regt.
2nd. Leinster Regt.	2nd. R. Dublin Fus.	7th. (SIH) R. Irish R.
1st. R. Munster Fus.	2nd. R. Munster Fus.	7/8th. R. Innis. Fus.

4. The Units to be received will arrive with complete transport, equipment and personnel, and will be kept intact. NO exchange of any of these categories will be allowed within the Division, and G.O's.C. Brigades will be held responsible that this is strictly carried out.

5. Instructions regarding Battalions to be broken up are as stated below, and the Battalions to be broken up will be notified by G.H.Q. from time to time. These notifications may be expected to be received at a very early date.

6. As far as possible the personnel of disbanded Battalions will be used to bring up to strength the remaining Battalions, as mentioned in para. 3.;
The surplus personnel not used for this purpose will be withdrawn to the Divl. Wing, under orders to be issued by the Division, and will be held as general reinforcements.

NOTE:- The Battalions actually to be broken up have been selected by G.H.Q. for certain territorial reasons, and to prevent the disbandment of Regular Battalions or Yeomanry Regiments.

7. G.H.Q., 3rd. Echelon will notify Division direct the Unit to be broken up, giving detailed instructions as to disposal of personnel, e.g, :-

P.T.O.

Specimen form of Order:-   -2-

Post From:- i.e. Bn. to be broken up.	Offrs.	O.R.	To include Regtl. Signlrs.	Post to:-
4th. Blankshires	15	290	8	2nd. Blankshires
	17	400	9	7th. Blankshires.

8.   On receipt of these orders O's. C. Battalions concerned will AT ONCE prepare nominal rolls (in triplicate) as follows :-

    (a) Officers & O.R. to be posted to (o.g.)2nd. Blankshires
    (b)   "   "   "   "   "   "   7th. Blankshires
    (c)   "   "   "   surplus when above postings have been carried out.

IMPORTANT NOTE:-
THE GREATEST CARE MUST BE EXERCISED IN THE COMPILATION OF ALL ROLLS, AS REGARDS CORRECT INITIALS, RANKS, CORRECT UNIT, RETL. NUMBER, ETC.

9.   One copy of the rolls referred to in para. 8 will be forwarded to Divisional H.Q., a second to G.H.Q.,3rd. Echelon, and the third copy will be handed to the Officer or Senior N.C.O. in charge of each party.

10.   These rolls will show any special qualifications possessed by Officers and O.R. so as to facilitate their re-employment in their new units.

11.   On receipt of these orders, all Officers and Other Ranks on the strength of Battalions which are to be amalgamated or disbanded will rejoin their Battalions, except those on leave or attending courses of instruction, or in the case of Officers Staff "Learners" as authorised by G.H.Q.

    Should any of the above not be immediately available to join the new Units to which they have been posted, nominal rolls will be rendered to this Office showing how each individual is employed.

12.   The names, ages and particulars of service of all surplus Quartermasters will be notified to Military Secretary this Office. Arrangements will be made by G.H.Q. to fill existing vacancies by the transfer of these surplus Quartermasters and to send the remainder home.

13.   The Headquarters of all Battalions (T.F. or Service) which are being broken up will be retained until all details connected with the disbandment have been settled, and the personnel will not be at the disposal of the Division for posting.

    When all postings have been carried out, this H.Q. Staff will be withdrawn to Corps Reinforcement Depots under arrangements to be notified from time to time.

(P.T.O. for para. 14.)

14. **LEAVE:-**

As leave is not to be stopped during reorganisation, nominal rolls will be forwarded to D.H.Q. by the Battalion being disbanded showing the particulars as stated below:-

(a) Names, Regtl. Nos. Ranks, etc. of all Offrs. & O.R. returning from leave or courses in the United Kingdom during the reorganisation period.
(b) Destination in each case, i.e. the Bn. to which Offr. or man should join.
(c) Date of return.
(d) Port of Disembarkation. NOTE:- Separate nominal rolls must be prepared for each Base Port.

THESE ROLLS WILL BE SUBMITTED TO THIS OFFICE IN DUPLICATE.

15. **Disposal of Funds:-**

The following procedure with regard to the disposal of Officers' and Sergeants' Messes, Canteen and other funds, will be adopted:-

(i) On receipt of this order, O's.C. Battalions concerned will take immediate steps to effect a settlement of all outstanding accounts. They will cause a balance sheet to be prepared.

(ii) In the case of Battalions absorbed into or amalgamated with other Battalions, the balance of such funds will be held on charge by the G.O.C. Division pending instructions from the A.G.

(iii) In the case of Battalions which are disbanded and cease to exist, the balance of all such funds will be remitted to the Command Paymaster, Base, for credit to the Public. A.O. 214 of 1916.)

16. **TRANSPORT AND STORES:-**

Regimental Transport of the Battalions to be disbanded will be disposed of as stated below, on receipt of further orders:-

* (a) 7th. Leinster Regt. to 24th. Division.
* (b) 10th. R. Dublin Fus. to 1st. Division.
  (c) 8/9th. R. Dublin Fus.)
  6th. R. Irish Regt.) Until further orders are received
  7/8th. R. Irish Fus.) from Q.M.G. this Transport complete
) will remain intact under the orders
) of Brigade Commanders, who will be
) held personally responsible that,
) (a) horses and vehicles are not
) exchanged with those of other units,
) (b) Horses are properly cared for
) and the vehicles maintained in ser-
) viceable condition ready for immed-
) iate use, and (c) The transport is
) not used to replace deficiencies in
) other units, & will not be shown as
) surplus on the "Surplus & Deficient
) H.T." return.

P.T.O. For continuation of para. 16.

-4-

* The Regimental Transport referred to will consist of the following :-

> Transport Officer and Sergeant.
> One Groom for every two Riding Horses.
> Transport Drivers with their horses and wagons complete and all wagon stores as in para. 4 of W.E. 483.

accessories

17. STORES:-

(i) As regards stores, other than transport equipment, the personnel of Battalions broken up, amalgamated or transferred will retain their accoutrements, steel helmets, box respirators and full scale of clothing and necessaries.

(ii) Arrangements will be made for Lewis Guns and their components to be returned to Army Gun Parks. Definite instructions will be issued later as regards this.

(iii) Special attention must be paid to the return of Lewis Guns and an explanation of any deficiencies in the establishment of Lewis Guns will be handed in with them.

(iv) Division will arrange to take over all S.A.A. Boxes on charge of Battalions when disbanded.

(v) Veterinary chests will be handed over to the O.C. Mobile Veterinary Section.

(vi) All other equipment will be returned to Railhead through D.A.D.O.S., where it will be checked by the R.O.O., and sent down to the Ordnance Depot supplying the Formation to which the Unit belongs.

SPECIAL NOTE:-

The nominal rolls referred to in para. 8. will include ALL Officers and O.R. on the effective strength of the Unit. Every man must be accounted for, whether he is serving with the Battalion or not.

[signature]

Lieut=Colonel,
A.A. & Q.M.G., 16th. Division.

31/1/18.

DISTRIBUTION:-

Each Inf. Bde.	5 copies.
"G"	1 copy.
Div. Train.	1 "
A.D.M.S.	1 "
D.A.D.V.S.	1 "
D.A.D.O.S.	1 "
Divl. Wing.	1 "

WAR DIARY.

FOR MONTH OF FEBRUARY, 1918.

VOLUME:- 24

UNIT:- 7th Btn Leinster Regiment.

Disbanded 23.2.18

WAR DIARY or INTELLIGENCE SUMMARY

Army Form C. 2118.

4th Bty. Leinster Regiment

(Erase heading not required.)

Place	Date	Hour	Summary of Events and Information	Remarks and references to Appendices
ST EMILIE	FEB 1st		D.T.R. handed over 1/Lt 200R at 8hrs for exchange to proceed in forward area.	
FRONT LINE	2nd		The Batt'n relieved 6th R.I. Regt according to COM 33 without incident at 8:30 p.m. 2/Lt Roy Ff. 2/Lt Roffe formed a covering screen in N.M.L during the relief.	(attached)
RIGHT SUB-SECT D.M.	3rd		OC quiet day. Double observers over hours the right. No found. 2 working parties of 1/Lt & 20 OR for revetting DUNCAN Av. and Braen Av.	
	4th		By night in hight alignment Bethynch pro-inity Bty refuging. Omend my day 6.30 p.m return CRO Crys. Ar. + park 8TB. Oct 10:10 p.m. a Party patrol sent out in advance of outside trench area encountered Inke no entered till 11.15 p.m. Six Off. & one man alone rob on S.O.S line. Two men were wounded by one rifle (no cars to which sent behind STORES TR. 2 OR. speed m 11:30 OR.	
	5th		From 5:0 am 6:30 a.m. an unusual lost to embarrassed but not First night 7th R 6 coming slight damage in several planes but no cars that in the enemy shelled working parties etc. 2 batteries of the 3rd were found & in addition	ind 3/ Lt F&D OR

WAR DIARY or INTELLIGENCE SUMMARY

Army Form C. 2118.

Place	Date	Hour	Summary of Events and Information	Remarks and references to Appendices
FRONT LINE	5th		Relief DOG Tr. between B.T. 7 & T. Coys. Battn. strength 21 offrs & 604 ORs.	
	6th		In the line, the day not including stragglers. Divided working parties to wire & those of the Bn were found. Coy much annoyed by enemy aerial artillery fire same disposition as on 2nd inst. Late in the afternoon an aeroplane reported the enemy supports to the North & Support Farm to be avoided. In consequence practically (?) fired 10 mins. Btn concentrations on these wires at 7.10 p.m. 8.30 p.m. 9 p.m. & 10.30 p.m. Enemy arty. retaliated lightly at 7.15 p.m. wounding one man & at 8.20 p.m. The other two shots were not replied to.	
	7th		A quiet day, 7 holidays nothing further being reported.	
	8th		This Battn. was relieved by the 2nd Battn., in accordance with O.O. No. 23 by 8.45 p.m. without incident and returned to Bde. Reserve in ST. EMILIE.	
BDE. RES.	9th		Coy. training, day spent in cleaning up.	
ST. EMILIE	10th		The Battn. attended morning service in VILLERS-FAUCON.	
	11th		Ch. party of 9 Offrs. & 200 ORs. carried out a 4 hours task digging a new trench grid M.9 ST. EMILIE. Collecting party of 2 NCOs & 40 ORs.	

WAR DIARY
or
INTELLIGENCE SUMMARY

Army Form C. 2118

Place	Date	Hour	Summary of Events and Information	Remarks and references to Appendices
	11th		Worked at Grand Fond during the afternoon. Approx was inspected prior to disbandment by Brig. Gen. H.Q. GRÉGOIRE at which he thanked personnel & officers on retention of the Battn's spirit and soaring behaviour. His working party of 3 offr & 200 O.Rs was retained and further party of 1 offr & 50 O.Rs provided in returning to Villers-Faucon.	
	12th		Yesterday's working parties repeated.	
	13th		The working parties of yesterday were repeated. The weather unsuitable transport set off by road to join 1st Div in afternoon.	
	14th		off 10am Lt. T.J. GLYNN-Dunn commanding the Battn. Entrainment. In charge of 3 offr, T.J. GLYNN Dunn & 200 O.Rs. Capt'y of 4 offr & 200 O.Rs again went into burying & clearing the Battn. No go still further offl'g up till to ROBIS T CONDE Then the Battn marched 2050 O.Rs marched to join the 2nd Bn in ROYSOY. and 2 Lt. SMYTHE. EC. North 2250 O.Rs proceeded to ROYSOY for march north	
	15th		off 8.30am a party of 2 offr & 120 O.Rs under Lt R.W. BOYES 11th HANTS PNRS. H.6 Purl. a Lurt party = 60 O.Rs under provided to join at 2nd Battn at ROYSOY.	
	16th		Returned to Dagsey's working Party provided to 2nd Battn.	
	17th		The Bn. H.Q. D.G.H. (Lieut. Col. J.D. MATHER cmdg) Capt. W.J. FARRELL. M.C. 2nd in Cmd. Capt. A.H. WHITEHEAD M.C. Acjt Cmd. Bn was at STANCOURT Reld proceeded to Camp at O.B.O.8.64. 1 unit hostile PÉRONNE	

A 5834 Wt. W4973 M687 750,000 8/16 D. D. & L. Ltd. Forms/C.2118/13.

WAR DIARY
or
INTELLIGENCE SUMMARY.

Army Form C. 2

(Erase heading not required.)

Instructions regarding War Diaries and Intelligence Summaries are contained in F. S. Regs., Part II. and the Staff Manual respectively. Title pages will be prepared in manuscript.

Place	Date	Hour	Summary of Events and Information	Remarks and references to Appendices
01.8.6.4	17th		Three recommendations were forwarded for the D.S.O. to 2.O.2. For 2.9.2. For Lieut and 243 O.R. and 12 Offrs	
	18th		Instructions were received for the field at B remaining the same. We are detailed to R 19th Entraining Billetry. No posts to function. It was decided that "D" Coy of the unit should be found by Leinsters and "A" "B" & "C" Coys should find all pickets and fire pickets on both sides, and should also patrol the areas shown on sheet issued by Command. "E" "F" & "G" Coys and 3rd Divl Cyclists under 2nd in Command to patrol urinhart, Chairman, Tower Trams, and Pollard Urquhart.	
	19th		The Captain who is at the one place but P.O Matilda in Reserve will go the one command of R 19th Ent. Det. is taking our officers at R Mr. Potter. Captain J.F. Dobson (Captain to Leinsters L.A.F.C.) and all remaining OR, (including 15) reviews instructing to proceed to L.L. I.B.D. Calais at flying up this party W/R Peronne by rail at 19 hour, en route in Calais via Amescamps and Boulogne.	
	20th		to train	
	21st & 22nd			
	22.30		Arrived Calais and reported to L.L. I.B.D. Officers from line and Regiment spent the Sgt. Mr. Officer and recovery in writing the R.L.L. until who could not be found were Count & Signatory together according to English.	O.N.O. with [illegible]

OPERATION ORDERS No XX 22.   Copy No. 12
by
Lt Col J.D. Mather
Commdg 7th Leinster Regt

                                                2nd Feb 1918
In the Field

1. The Battalion will relieve the 6th ROYAL IRISH REGT in the right sub-section on the evening of the 2nd inst.

2. On completion of relief the disposition of the Battn will be as follows:

   "A" Coy Front line Left, relieving "C" Coy R.I.Regt.
   "B" Coy Front Line Right relieving "D" Coy   "
   "C" Coy Reserve in KEN LANE   "   "A" Coy   "
   "D" Coy Support in   "   "B" Coy   "
            DUNCAN POST
   Bn H.Qrs KEN LANE F.17.a.3.1.

3. The Battn will march out of present shelters at 5.0pm in the above order by route used when last relieved in line, and will be met by 2 guides per Coy and one from Battn H.Qrs at F.16.c.8.1. at 6.30pm. 200 yds. interval between platoons will be maintained.

4. Lewis Guns of A & B Coys will be loaded in Limber at Level Crossing at 3.30pm and proceed to 5 X Roads where they will be met by their No 1s at 4.30pm. One Lewis Gun team of "C" Coy will be attached to "A" Coy and will be loaded on the same limber.
Remainder of Lewis Guns will move with the Battn.

5. Advance Parties consisting of 1 Officer 1 Senior N.C.O. 4 L.Guns No 1s and Gas N.C.O. per Coy with the Intelligence Officer, Signals Sergt, 1 Linesman and 1 N.C.O. from Battn H.Qrs will parade at Orderly Room at 9.30am to proceed to take over.

6. A Patrol party of 1 Officer and 15 other ranks from A.&.B Coys with the Intelligence officer and 10 Battn Scouts will parade with advance party. Arrangements for patrols to cover relief will be made by Battalion Intelligence Officer.

7. The following will be taken over:- (a) Trench Stores, (b) written Defence Scheme (c) all documents connected with the Line (d) work in progress & proposed (in writing) Trench stores to be at Orderly Room by 1st Runner Post, 3rd instant.

8. TRANSPORT. Blankets(neatly rolled in bundles of 10) and packs will be stacked at Level Crossing by 9.0 a.m. Officers' Kits, & Coy. Stores, Mobile Reserve of Ammunition, etc. for transport Lines to be ready by noon.
   One Lewis Gun Limber will be at Level Crossing at 3.15 p.m.
   One   "   "   "   "   "   "   "   "   " 4.45 p.m.
   Maltese Cart, Mess cart, & one Limber to be at Battn. H.Qrs. at 5.0 p.m. Spring Cart to collect Coy. Mess Kits at 4.30 p.m.

9. Present shelters to be handed over by Quartermaster. Coy. Commdrs. will see that they are left in a clean and sanitary condition, and render usual certificate to this effect.
   Battalion H.Qrs. will also be handed over by Quartermaster.

10. COMPLETION OF RELIEF to be reported by code message "NIL RETURN"

                                (sd) A. H. WHITEHEAD.Capt & Adjt.
                                     7th Bn. Leinster Regt,.

Copies to:- (1) Commdg. Officer. (5) O.C. "C" Coy. (9) Signals Officer.
            (2) Adjutant.   (6) "   "D" " (10) 47th I. Bde.
            (3) O.C. "A" Coy.   (7) Quartermaster.(11) 6th R.I.Regt.
            (4) "   "B" "   (8) Transport Offr(12) War Diary.
                        (13) Retained.

SECRET.   Copy No. 13

OPERATION ORDER, No. 23.

by

Lt. Col. J. T. MATHER,
Commdg. 7th LEINSTER REGT.,

In the Field.   7th February, 1918.

I. THE Battalion will be relieved in the Right sub-section by the 2ND LEINSTER REGIMENT on 8th February, 1918.

II. ON relief, the Battalion will proceed via F 16 d, 45.25, F 16 c, 8.1., - F 21 a, 7.2½, and RONSSOY - ST. EMILIE Road to Brigade Reserve at ST. EMILIE.

   Disposition will be as follows:-

   A. B. C. D. Coys. in Railway Cutting, E 23 d.
   Headquarters at E 24 a, 8.1.

   All movement will be by platoon, at 500 yards' interval.

III. THE Shelters at ST. EMILIE and Battalion Headquarters will be taken over from the 6TH CONNAUGHT RANGERS by the Quartermaster. C.Q.M.Sgts will meet companies on arrival.

IV. GUIDES. (a) 1 Guide from each front line company will meet incoming Lewis Gun teams at F 16 d, 45, 25, at 3.0 p.m.
   (b) 1 Guide from each front-line company will meet incoming patrol parties at F 16 d, 45.25. at 3.30 p.m. (The above Guides will report to 2nd Lt. O'BRIEN at Battn. Headquarters at 2.30 p.m.)
   (c) 1 Guide per company, and one for Battn. H.Qrs. will report to 2nd LT. O'BRIEN at Battn. H. Qrs. at 3.30 p.m. and proceed to meet incoming unit at F 16 d, 45.25 at 5.15 p.m.
   (d) 1 Guide from Platoon at BASSE BOULOGNE SOUTH will report to O.C., "D" Coy. 2ND LEINSTER REGIMENT, at SANDBAG LANE, RONSSOY, at 5.30 p.m.

V. TRENCH STORES, and Work in Progress, and Proposed, will be handed over on relief, and a Certificate of Cleanliness obtained.
   Trench Stores lists, and Certificates, to be at Orderly Room by 10. 0 a.m. 9th instant.

VI. TRANSPORT. Lewis Gun Limbers will be at 5 X Roads, F 16 d, 45.25. at 5.30 p.m. Spring Cart (for Company Messes) and Maltese Cart, will be at DUNCAN POST at 5.0 p.m. Mess cart and one Limber will be at Battalion Headquarters at 5.30 p.m.

VII. COMPLETION OF RELIEF to be reported to Battalion Headquarters by Code Word "LAST"; arrival in Billets to be immediately reported by Runner to Headquarters.

                                    (sgd.) A. H. WHITEHEAD. Capt & Adjt.
                                           7th Leinster Regiment.

Copies to:- (1) Commdg. Officer. (6) O.C. "D" Coy.   (11) 2nd Leinster Regt.
            (2) Adjutant.   (7) Quartermaster.   (12) 6th Connaught Rgrs.
            (3) O.C. A. Coy.   (8) Transport Off.   (13) War Diary.
            (4) "   B. "   (9) Signals Officer (14) Retained.
            (5) "   C. "   (10) 47th I. Bde.

OFFICERS AND MEN OF THE 7TH LEINSTER REGIMENT.

In a very few days, the Battalion will cease to exist as a unit, but its spirit will go marching on.

The Battalion was raised in Ireland, at the Nation's call for help, and the generous, noble-spirited Irishman responded to the Call, and right nobly has the Battalion done its work

Don't dream for a minute that the extreme exigencies of the Service and the 7TH LEINSTER REGIMENT. Its proud record, from LOOS to CROISILLES HEIGHTS, that never a German has entered its line, and that it has always fulfilled every call made upon it, will live for ever ! - and every member of that glorious band which left Ireland on the Third of September, 1915, with those who have come since to maintain the unbroken success of its record, will not be forgotten.

Your children, grand-children, unto the last generations, will tell with pride not only of the great and noble deeds of the 7th LEINSTERS, but, of the brilliant and heroic deeds of the individuals of the BATTALION.

The Battalion which many of you are joining, has also done brilliantly during the war; so, always do in it as you have done in the SEVENTH, and you have nothing to fear.

This war is rapidly coming to a close, perhaps sooner than most of us imagine, and I wish you all good fortune, and hope that you will soon be re-united with your dear ones back in the Old Country.

Your Motto will rest firm in the care of the whole Army, as "EVERYWHERE, AND ALWAYS, FAITHFUL."

---------- O ----------

www.ingramcontent.com/pod-product-compliance
Lightning Source LLC
Chambersburg PA
CBHW081354160426
43192CB00013B/2402